Dance Sense

Dance Sense

Theory and Practice for Dance Students

SECOND EDITION

Linda Ashley

Northcote House

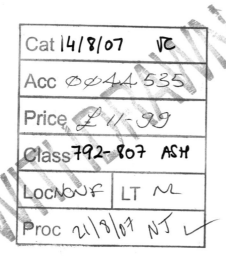
© Copyright 2005 by Linda Ashley

Published by Northcote House Publishers Ltd,
Horndon House, Horndon, Tavistock,
Devon PL19 9NQ, United Kingdom
Tel: (01822) 810066. Fax: (01822) 810034.

First edition 1997
Reprinted 2000
Reprinted 2002

Second edition 2005

British Library Cataloguing-in-Data
A catalogue record for this book is available from the British Library.

ISBN 0 7463 1156 7

Typeset by TW Typesetting, Plymouth, Devon
Printed and bound in Great Britain by Baskerville Press Ltd, Salisbury

To my parents

CONTENTS

ILLUSTRATIONS

FOREWORD

A NOTE FOR TEACHERS

This is a text for younger dance students (eg GCSE) although parts of it may also be found appropriate for use with students both above and below this level. It has been written with the needs of inexperienced dance students in mind and I hope it will be used beneficially with them as part of a teaching programme linked to the practical tasks I have included, as well as the examples of choreography, the illustrations and the suggested videos. I hope it will also provide many structured ideas for homework supplemented by teacher-guided reading, which places dance in a practical context and encourages an appreciation of other dance works.

While covering all the main elements of the revised GCSE Dance syllabus it should prove flexible enough to allow a coursework programme to be built around it.

This second edition includes the many recent additions to the syllabus. They bring extra breadth and depth to dance studies and include: safe studio and personal practice; expressive skills; more European and international genres and professional works; videodance, online and IT; lighting; work of prominent choreographers with particular relevance to the GCSE syllabus such as Lea Anderson.

It also relates more directly to (and sources) varied resources such as videos, dvds, texts, web sites and music. These are greater in number and more easily available globally nowadays.

In the final chapter tasks are related to the (UK) Key Skills, so that they may be tracked easily into dance studio practice. These have similar equivalents in many countries and can be easily adapted.

The book is designed to be used selectively in class rather than worked through slavishly from cover to cover.

FOR THE STUDENT

This book is for you. I hope that first and foremost you enjoy using it and secondly that it helps you to further your understanding of dance. Finally, I hope it helps you to enjoy to the full the fascinating world of dance performance, choreography and appreciation.

ACKNOWLEDGEMENTS

I am greatly indebted to all my family, friends and colleagues near and far who give me advice, support and encouragement in my work. Some of you I may not have seen for several years, but you are in my thoughts often as I write and in this way you provide valuable substance. Others of you far away have provided important comment and ideas. I thank all of you most sincerely.

For those of you nearer to my present home, heartfelt thanks for all your sharing, caring support. Of course all of this and more should be said of my loving husband Michael. One day we really will retire and perhaps run a goldfish farm.

I would like to acknowledge all the dancers, students and children with whom I have worked over the years. Their enthusiasm and ideas have been a rich source of inspiration to me.

I am most grateful for support from the following: Sarah Woodcock and her staff at the Theatre Museum; Francesca Franchi at the Royal Opera House; Jayne Pritchard, archivist for Rambert Dance Company and English National Ballet; London Contemporary Dance Theatre; Chris Nash; The Laban Centre Library; Erica Stanton and Jane Quinn; Catherine Ashmore; Cloud Gate Dance Theatre of Taiwan, Pei-Yun Chen; The New York Public Library; Phil Karg and Tom Lisanti; Royal New Zealand Ballet, Kirsten Dennis; Li Gai Farandole, Guillaume Longuet.

The author and the publishers gratefully acknowledge the following for supplying illustrations and granting permission for their use. Catherine Ashmore (plates 1.8, 3.5, 5.3, 7.3); British Museum, London (plates 1.1, 1.2, 1.3); Cloud Gate Dance Theatre of Taiwan (plates 2.7 photographer Yu Hui-hung, 7.1 and 7.5 photographer Liu Chen-hsiang); Bill Cooper (plate 7.4); Anthony Crickmay (plates 2.5, 3.2, 3.3); Hugo Glendinning (plate 8.3) with thanks to Erica Bolton and Jane Quinn. James Klosty (plate 3.7); Eleni Leoussi (plate 5.8) with thanks to Arts Administration.

Chapter 1

A HISTORY OF DANCE

Throughout this book there are photographs and examples of dance from history to the present day. This chapter does not cover the history of all dance forms in society: to do so would need a separate book.

What follows gives some idea of how we arrived at where we are now. What events in the past led to you reading this book? Where did the dance that we see at the theatre today originate? What are its influences from the past?

THE EVOLUTION OF DANCE

Dance in Early Times

Dance is found among all peoples of the world, indeed, some say that it is the oldest art form. Today, as in earlier communities, dance is still an important part of social and religious life. Social occasions such as birth, death, harvest, coming-of-age, and healing are marked by dancing in order to maintain the wellbeing of the community.

Whether in Africa, Asia, Europe, America or the Pacific symbolic movement is used where speech alone may not be enough. The intricate hand gestures or *mudras* of Indian dance are an example of this. The power of movement can say more than many words. The sun, moon, stars, seasons, animals, all influence the rituals and dances of these communities and create powerful beliefs and incredible physical feats. A *Sufi* dervish spinning for twelve or fifteen hours without dizziness, an Indonesian trance dancer thrusting knives onto a bare chest so strongly that the blades bend, are just two examples.

In Europe ancient ceremonies are still to be found even though the original pagan dances have long since been Christianised or have disappeared altogether. In Barcelona you can still see the Catalonians perform their national circle dance, the *Sardana*. This is a symbol of their identity and was banned on threat of imprisonment under the government of General Franco, such was its power! In eastern Europe too, where an agricultural lifestyle is still dominant, there are many customs such as carnival processions with animal masks and decorative costume to celebrate the arrival of spring. In Bulgaria one dance features women dancing around a barrel, jumping as high as possible to make the crops grow. In Britain the Morris dance is the ghost of early fertility rites.

The prehistoric cave paintings in France, the Balkans and the Middle East depict dances in lines and circles. Our first real knowledge of dance comes from the early civilizations of Sumeria, Assyria, Egypt and Greece. These people left written records and art objects which show clearly processions and ritual dances to their deities. Dancers were trained in order to perform in the many acts of worship, like the dance of stars which was based on the movements of the solar system and supposedly influenced rain, crops and survival. Gradually dancing became a profession for entertaining the upper classes. Similar processes happened in ancient Greece, but here dance was also part of education. Plato wrote 'to sing and dance well is to be well educated.'

In ancient Rome life was lived to the full and rituals became excessive. Dance did not escape abuse, and it was therefore hardly surprising that the early Christians associated dance with their persecution and suffering. Throughout the Dark and Middle Ages dance was disapproved of and discouraged. As Christianity spread through Europe dance was only allowed if it was based on a holy theme. This resulted in dance being performed in the churches. Often pagan festivals were still celebrated, masked as Christian holy days with churches built on top of existing pagan shrines.

Such unusual dances as *The Dance of Death* and weird *Danseomania* spread from the seventh century through to the fifteenth century, still showing their pagan roots. So the peasants continued to dance in circles, chains and couples to be copied and refined by the nobility. Even today in Spain, *Bal de la Mort* is still danced during Holy Week. Twelve men and three women dress in black on which skeletons are painted and they process the town to the sound of a single drum.

The Birth of Ballet

In castles and palaces across Europe the nobility feasted and dance flourished. The first dancing masters appeared in Italy in the 1400s. The

1.1 Relief of Dancing Girls in Thebes c. 1500–1400 BC

1.2 Terracotta relief 1st century AD. A maenad and a satyr dance with the infant Dionysos

Italian word *ballere* means 'to dance' and is the word from which ballet is derived. Extravagant spectacles were held akin to our modern day nightclub cabaret, telling myths and legends and stories of important events. Dancing masters appeared and set standards of etiquette. All the gentlemen were expected to be accomplished dancers.

By the end of the 1500s dancing was high fashion at the courts of Europe and so ballet was born. At this time, the typical upright carriage of the body, turn-out, the five positions and the basic steps were developed by the Italian and French aristocracy. By the 1600s ballet was performed in actual theatres, allowing the audience to see it from the front. This separation of performer and viewer led to the professional form of ballet as we now know it.

The opening of the Paris Opera Ballet School in 1713 guaranteed the development of choreographer, principal dancer and *corps de ballet*. The coming of the Romantic era from about 1830 gave rise to such famous works as *La Sylphide* (1832) by Filippo Taglioni for his daughter Marie Taglioni and August Bournonville's version in 1836 for the Royal Danish Ballet which still survives today. The training of dancers was also evolving and the nineteenth century innovation of dancing *en pointe* emphasised the romantic 'heavenly' nature of ballet.

Eventually a combination of the Franco-Prussian war and excessive decadence led ballet into decline. Standards of choreography and technique declined. This was to be the end of Paris as the leader in the world of ballet.

Russia to the Rescue

Russia always copied European trends and fashions and ballet was no exception. In 1766 it received royal patronage and in 1847 French born Marius Petipa moved to St Petersburg and stayed there for almost 60 years. Ballet thrived in Russia, and was still quite respectable at a time when in Europe it was considered morally questionable. Petipa was producing choreography of large ballets with great variety in styles tinged with a new sort of toughness. His production of the *Sleeping Beauty* (1890), was outstanding in its beauty and demanded all the skills of the excellent dancers from the Imperial School. In 2000 it was reconstructed by the Kirov ballet from the original notation. It was much longer than more modern versions because many of the lost mime scenes were reinstated.

1.3 Court and rustic dance. Sixteenth-century engraving by Theodor de Bry

1.4 Marie Taglioni

1.5 The six fairies from the Diaghilev Ballet production of THE SLEEPING
PRINCESS *(1921) choreography Bronislava Nijinska*

By the early twentieth century Russian ballet was technically the best
but its creativity declined until Mikhel Fokine began to work in St
Petersburg. He questioned the old ways and formulas and introduced
new ideas. He moved in artistic circles which brought him in contact with
entrepreneur Serge Diaghilev who was to become director of the new
ballet company of which Fokine would be the principal choreographer.

Task 1

Watch a video of *Les Sylphides* (1909), choreography Mikhel Fokine
for Imperial Ballet Theatre, Russia, music by Chopin. Notice and
explain the following:
1. How do the movements of the dance give it a romantic look?
2. What kind of group shapes and patterns do the *corps de ballet* use?

The New Approach

Diaghilev decided to export Russian ballet to the rest of Europe. In 1910
he showed off Fokine's *Firebird* set to Stravinsky's music and
Schéhérazade (music, Rimsky-Korsakof) with Leon Bakst's sumptuous
set and costumes. The Paris audience was won over, seeing a refreshing

1.6 Nijinsky in SCHÉHÉRAZADE *(1910)*

mix of expression of complex feelings, strong male dancing and unity of style, music and visual setting. So Diaghilev's 'Ballets Russes' was taken out of Russia and with it many famous dancers such as Pavlova and Karsavina. Famous composers like Prokofiev and Debussy, artists like Bakst and Benois and choreography not only from Fokine but Vaslav Nijinsky, Leonide Massine, Bronislava Nijinska and George Balanchine all collaborated in this ballet revival.

Fokine was considered to be the father of modern ballet. In his footsteps came Vaslav Nijinsky – dancer extraordinary with his soaring jumps who was also encouraged by Diaghilev to choreograph. His *L'Après Midi d'un Faune* (1912) outraged Parisian audiences in its overt symbolism, regarded by its audience as obscene. His *Le Sacré du Printemps* (1913) (Stravinsky) caused a riot because of its unconventional score depicting a pagan ritual, with its use of uneven rhythmic pounding and off-beat accents.

The company continued to work until Diaghilev's death in 1929. His dancers and choreographers left to carry the legacy to new parts of the world. Artists such as George Balanchine travelled as far away as the USA.

In Britain Marie Rambert and Ninette de Valois built on Diaghilev's policy and started to build a British 'ballet club'. Names such as Alicia Markova, Margot Fonteyn, Antony Tudor and Frederick Ashton formed the beginnings of the Ballet Rambert (1935) and the Royal Ballet (originally Vic-Wells Ballet 1931), now two of Britain's leading companies. In 1966 the now renamed Rambert Dance Company became more of a modern dance company, featuring works in the Graham style by Norman Morrice and Glen Tetley. Later, under directors John Chesworth and Robert North this tendency became more pronounced. From 1986 under the direction of Richard Alston, the Cunningham influence dominated. Christopher Bruce became director in 1994 and it returned to a more traditional modern style with works such as his own *Four Scenes* (1998) and *Ghost Dances* (1981). Neoclassical style dances, from such choreographers as Jiri Kylian, were also included in the repertoire.

Similarly, in 1926 Dame Ninette de Valois, with help from theatre owner Lilian Bayliss, brought ballet back to the Sadler's Wells Theatre. The first performance starred Alicia Markova and Anton Dolin to be followed later by Margot Fonteyn and Robert Helpmann. In 1935, after

1.7 LES RENDEZVOUS (1933) choreography Frederick Ashton

having worked with Rambert, Frederick Ashton joined as choreographer. In 1956 Sadler's Wells received a Royal Charter and became known as the 'Royal Ballet'. It started a touring section in addition to the main body. In 1963 Ashton became director, passing to Kenneth Macmillan in 1970. Throughout the focus was on English choreography and the classics. Typical of these works were Ashton's light-hearted and witty *Façade* (1931) to music by William Walton and the simple rural frolics of *La Fille Mal Gardée* (1960). He also revived Nijinska's *Les Noces* (1923) and made work for the partnership of Fonteyn and Rudolf Nureyev. Under Macmillan the focus was the same but with more emphasis on full length dance-dramas like *Mayerling* (1978) and more modern classical work like Tetley's plotless *Gemini* (1977). Under Norman Morrice's directorship, Sadler's Wells Royal Ballet emphasised the modern style. Then in 1986 ex-dancer Anthony Dowell took over and continued to use fewer guest choreographers and to encourage in-house work. Home-grown choreographers such as Ashley Page and David Bintley featured regularly alongside a staple of well-loved classics and full-length works like Macmillan's *The Prince of the Pagodas* (1989) to music by Benjamin Britten. Australian Ross Stretton became director in 2001 but resigned in 2002. At the time of writing assistant director Monica Mason is the new director.

In 1990 part of the company moved to new premises and is now known as the Birmingham Royal Ballet. The Diaghilev legacy was thus developed in Great Britain to become a distinctive British style of ballet performed by a strong modern company with a tradition of nurturing young choreographers, musicians and artists.

THE MODERN DANCE ERA

As Diaghilev and his associates were revolutionising the ballet other rebels were appearing with ideas and approaches that had little to do with that world. In the United States of America the accepted form of ballet was being rejected by the dancers themselves who wanted to find their own ways of moving.

Loie Fuller was known for her dances using skirts and scarves in coloured light. As the electric light was the discovery of the time this gave her show exotic glitter and interest. She was shadowed eventually by the untrained genius of Isadora Duncan who, as an outspoken feminist, believed in a woman's right to love and bear her children as she pleased. This would have been a scandalous opinion at the time. She dared to dance in the face of America's puritan heritage and she shocked everyone with her use of flimsy, loose clothes, bare feet, simple improvisation, bare stage and her ambitious use of classical 'greats' such as the music of Beethoven and Wagner. Her lone, liberal free-spirit won acclaim in Europe and America, and set a path for others to follow.

At the same time Ruth St Denis trod the boards with spontaneity and individuality. For her, a cigarette advertisement showing an Egyptian goddess inspired her own style of dance which was exotic and mysterious. She met Ted Shawn in 1914 who was first her pupil and later husband. Together they formed the company Denishawn and offered classes in Spanish, Oriental, American-Indian dance and ballet. One of their students was Martha Graham. Later Shawn formed the first all-male company, setting a path for others to follow.

By the time of the Great Depression the exotic gave way to a hardening of feeling. Martha Graham was very serious in making hard-edged dance technique and choreography as described in later chapters. Its importance lies in its point of view, that is, that the individual choreographer is a priority. It is not merely a technique or a date that makes 'modern dance'. Graham rebelled against Denishawn just as Duncan had against ballet. So in the early 1920s and 30s dance began to metamorphose into a new look.

In America and Germany where ballet had little prestige, modern dancers experimented relentlessly. The resultant look was often hard, stark and earthy, and usually the work of women as society reeled from the perfume of the romantic ballet which labelled male dancing as effeminate. Women like Martha Graham, Doris Humphrey, Hanya Holm and Mary Wigman announced their independence from traditional thought, preferring to be known as women and artists through their work. Interestingly, men of the time who were associated with dance were often initially associated with music or acting and found their way to dance via these other forms. Such men were Emile Jacques-Dalcroze and Rudolf Laban whose analytical theories informed the work of Wigman and Holm. As a result of the Second World War dance in Germany faded, but the ideas were passed on to the United States by Hanya Holm who stayed there and continued to develop the principles along lines which suited the American temperament, physique and culture.

Meanwhile in Britain important advances were being made in dance education as Rudolf Laban, exiled by the war, introduced his theories into the world of modern educational dance. Perhaps you are reading this book as part of your studies in dance. If so, you are a part of the legacy of Laban. He was the leader of the Central European school of modern dance and his work embraced many areas from his well-known system of dance notation *Labanotation*, to his movement choirs *Bewegungschore*, the pure expression of human involvement in the dance of the cosmos. His pupils and collaborators were many and included Kurt Jooss and Lisa Ullmann. He also worked on analysing movement in industrial processes. By the 1950s modern dance was established but there was more to follow. The early pioneers gave rise to another generation of choreographers; Paul Taylor, Eric Hawkins and Alwin Nikolais to name just a few, who each had their own distinctive styles. Not least was a pupil of Martha Graham called Merce Cunningham who maintained the tradition of the new by producing controversial and challenging dance that announced yet another revolution to challenge dance audiences.

Merce Cunningham was a dancer with Graham but he developed his ideas which conflicted with hers. Insisting that dance is only about dancing and developing a new technique to express his idea he took dance into the next era.

His technique combined almost balletic footwork with rapid shifts of weight and direction, a mobile spine and cascading rhythms. As well as this, his use of chance methods to construct dances, his attitude to the stage space being an open, many-sided area and his idea that movement, music and set are independent of each other (often only coming together for the first time in performance) reflect his associations with other art forms. Composer John Cage and artists like Andy Warhol and Robert Rauschenberg would be his fellow conspirators in the forming of radical ideas that, even though first rejected, are now a part of the mainstream of dance. Cunningham's dances are now in the repertoires of Rambert Dance Company and New York City Ballet amongst many.

Martha Graham, too, was to have a worldwide significance, and in Britain in the 1960s hotelier Robin Howard was so impressed by her work that he set up a trust to allow her technique to be taught in London. The chosen director was ex-Graham dancer Robert Cohan and so in 1967 the London Contemporary Dance Theatre was formed. It has given birth to several of Britain's leading choreographers including Siobahn Davies and Richard Alston. Through touring, workshops and residencies a massive new audience was created for contemporary dance in Britain. For a long time Cohan's style, softer than that of Graham, but still full of movement with meaning, was most obvious in the company's performances. Examples are the humorous *Waterless Method of Swimming Instruction* (1974), the haunting *Cell* (1969) and the lyrical, biblical *Stabat Mater* (1975). After Cohan's retirement in 1989, a series of directors ran the company maintaining its American 'look'. In 1996 it became the Richard Alston Dance Company and the style changed to a mix of Cunningham and post modern Release styles.

Task 2

Watch excerpts from the following videos; Robert North, *Death and the Maiden* (1980); Richard Alston, *Soda Lake* (1981); Christopher Bruce, *Sergeant Early's Dream* (1984). Answer the following questions:

1. Which of the three is concerned more with Graham's idea of movement that has meaning and which is concerned with movement for its own sake?
2. Which shows a Graham style of movement and which does not? Describe the style of one which is *not* in a Graham style.
3. What is the content of each?
4. How does each of them use accompaniment and how does it help to make the expression clearer?

AFTER THE MODERN

The post modern dance genre began its rich era of experiment when in New York in the 1960s even Cunningham was thought of as too restricted. As ever, dance responded to more general trends in society. The decade represented challenge to any and all authority: young people questioned civil rights, the Vietnam war, sexual liberation, the law and demanded to be 'free'. Young dancers questioned the need for technique, seeing it as being too rigid and they asked the ultimate question 'what *is* dance?' This gave rise to exploration in every direction.

1.8 OPAL LOOP *(1989) choreography Trisha Brown, for Rambert Dance Company*

In 1962 the co-operative group the Judson Dance Theatre began. Most of them were from the Cunningham studio and company, and they rebelled against the existing *avant-garde* to form another one! Names like Trisha Brown, Yvonne Rainer, Steve Paxton, David Gordon decided that technique was too limiting, abandoned the trained bodies of dancers, made all decisions which affected the group collectively and rejected the proscenium stage and repertory. They were interested in everyday movement rather than that which was theatricalised and therefore – in their eyes – artificial, and they used non-dancers in their work. Dance appeared on rooftops, in parks, streets and museums. Others were to bring modern dance and ballet closer and rejected the gender stereotypes attached to dance which they regarded as being limiting and unjust. Dancers appeared naked to make the point that gender and nudity were not important.

The world of painting was exploring similar issues, for example using pedestrian objects like the soup cans of Andy Warhol. The 'Happenings' of the sixties emphasised spontaneity, natural movement, audience participation, basically anything 'far-out' and the further out the better! This, of course, can only echo the radical work of Isadora Duncan and her belief in the truth of only what is natural. In some ways a circle was being completed.

Prior to this the only traditions which had maintained touch with improvisation were those in the Central European Expressionist style, the tradition of Hanya Holm and her students. However, in Europe itself one individual, Pina Bausch, trod new ground in the steps of the Central European style. A direct descendant of the Laban-Jooss school, she replaced deeper emotions into movement and performance. Her work reveals the stark reality of twentieth century life, its isolation, violence, humour, horror and psychoanalysis. Her influence spread all over Europe.

In Britain the flagship in the 1970s of the post modern movement was New Dance. Later such companies as DV8 led by Lloyd Newson reveal interest in issues of sexual politics as well as the darkness of the Bausch/European style. Other exponents show a typical wide variety of approaches. The minimal repetition and calm contemplation of Rosemary Butcher's work contrasts with that of the Cholmondeleys which is full of wry humour, feminist strategy and rich in unusual gesture.

Similarly dance by Motionhouse and Laurie Booth builds on Steve Paxton's approach and his style of contact improvisation. There is also concern that dance should be for everyone whatever age, race or disability. Fergus Early started a community dance group in 1987. *Green Candle* aimed to provide opportunity for everyone to dance as their birthright. Originally trained at the Royal Ballet School and danced with the Royal Ballet, his direction hung a sharp left turn when, in 1976, he co-founded X6 dance collective. He now runs dance projects which involve the elderly and others with special needs. Similarly *CandoCo* started in 1991, using contact improvisation style and techniques to draw together both disabled and non-disabled dancers;

'Central to the company's teaching is the principal of listening through touch . . . By learning to listen, students gain information

about their own and their partner's ways of moving and an understanding of each other's strengths and weaknesses.'[1]

Task 3

Watch the following videos by Motionhouse: *The House of Bones* or *Different Dancers Similar Motion*. As you watch note down answers to the following questions:

1. How is the movement style characteristic of post modern dance?
2. When and where was this style first discovered and by whom?
3. Why is working with groups who have special needs typical of post modern dance?

Task 4

Research an issue of concern like homelessness, child abuse, caring for the environment and discuss it in a group. From improvisation make a short group dance. Find suitable accompaniment and a title.

Various companies have, and still do, work under this umbrella and indeed a whole annual event called *Dance Umbrella* promotes new dance every November. Even though it is centred in London it stages events all over the UK and as well as performance it includes video, film, online and digital work, open discussions, leaving room for the ongoing exchange of opinion which is the very lifeblood of such a style. In Britain today we see many examples of dances from other countries such as India and Africa which have morphed in the new context of a different culture. Shobana Jeyasingh, a Bharatha Natyam dancer, and other classical Indian dancers, have developed the style of South Asian dance by including techniques of post modern work such as contact improvisation. Pan-African dance styles have similarly evolved. The work of Adzido, founded in 1984 by Ghanaian George Dzikunu and Emmanuel Tagoe is now Europe's largest touring African dance company. It presents pan African classic dances usually within a story form. Adzido have a large education programme of workshops and projects to make

---

[1] *Candoco Education pack.*

their music and dance accessible to British audiences. A thought-provoking comment comes from from David Henshaw:

'Black dance theatre is, perhaps, only a transitional concept, acceptable as a bridge to an homogeneous dance culture reflecting all sections of an inclusive European community.'[2]

This multi-cultural melting-pot is a global phenomenon. The Internet, satellite tv and jet travel bring cultures into frequent close contact. Cultures have always influenced each other, but perhaps this is speeded up nowadays. British based choreographer Mark Baldwin recently returned to his native New Zealand to make a work which collaborated with the Maori group *Te Matarae I Orehu*, choreographer Wetini Mitai-Ngatai. This full evening work *Ihi FrENZy* (2001) was accompanied by Kiwi pop legends Split ENZ and mixed the genres of Maori kapa haka, ballet, jazz and modern into a post modern soup. In France, Belgium and Holland names like Maguy Marin, Anne Teresa De Keersmaeker, Maurice Béjart, Jiri Kylian, Hans van Manen and Philippe Decouflé represent some diverse modern and post modern developments. In France Decouflé follows on from the modern dance tradition of American Alwin Nikolais who had studied within the European expressionist style of Hanya Holm. A very complex 'family history' this one! Nikolais worked in a style of total dance theatre where dance, lights, costumes and props merged into a kaleidoscope effect, being difficult to tell where the humans started and the physical setting ended. The French government invited him to form the Centre National de Danse Contemporaine in 1978 where, after circus school and mime with Marcel Marceau, Decouflé was later to study. These various influences result in a French post modern style, dreamlike and surreal, full of theatricality, parody and humour quoting on past styles, popular culture and high art.

OTHER DANCE GENRES, CULTURES AND FORMS

Up until now this chapter has focused on the history of the main dance genres such as ballet and modern dance. The final part will turn its attention to other aspects of dance in contemporary society.

---

[2] *Black Attitudes*, in *Dance Theatre Journal*, vol. 8 no. 4, Spring 1991.

1.9 *Royal New Zealand Ballet and Te Matarae I Orehu performing* Ihi FrENZy

West End shows like *Cats* and *Starlight Express* are the commercial end of the dance spectrum. A very well-known example of such work is the musical *Chorusline* where the jazz dance style powerfully hits the beat. Jazz dance styles such as those of Matt Mattox and Bob Fosse are highly suited to the glitter and glamour of the commercial theatre.

The history of jazz dance is rooted in African rhythms brought to the USA with the slave trade in the early 1800s. In the deep south of the United States black slaves created jazz music and the movements to go with it. Movements consisted of a great deal of twisting and wiggling of the hips in a spontaneous fashion and continued to develop with the music into a mix of European and African styles.

Later it developed into crazes of such social dances as tango, rumba, samba and of course the charleston. The African legacy of hip gyration, low bent stance, rippling spine and limbs reacting to the beat of the drums was here to stay.

A style of show dance was born as a way for poor black people of America to make a little money, whether on street corners or in the shows (as depicted in the film *The Cotton Club*). Tap dance was, and still is, a popular entertaining genre. Dancers like Katherine Dunham and Pearl Primus researched African and Carribean dances and adapted them into jazz and modern genres for stage. Gradually jazz became a recognised system of technical training, differing with the style of the teacher and known for its physically demanding exercises.

American tap dance blended African styles with the European clog dances and Irish jigs, reels and step dancing. Fred Astaire showed clearly the European tap style, an upright carriage of the torso combined with a smoother, less bouncy look than the American style. Another 'great', Gene Kelly, blended jazz style with a more black influenced tap. The stage musical *42nd Street* is typical of the white American style. It is interesting to note here that much black talent would never have become known because of the racism of those times, if it were not for such shows. An old film, *Stormy Weather* (1943), is well worth searching out to see the high quality of dancing from the all-black cast.

In Britain these styles of jazz and tap dance now form a backbone of stage shows. The musical *Stepping Out* by Richard Harris has done much to popularise tap since the decline of Hollywood films. It follows events in the lives of a ladies' (and one man) tap dancing class. And always remember, Ginger Rogers did everything Fred Astaire did but backwards *and* in high heels! The spectacular *Riverdance* reveals the historical mix of cultures. An updated style of tap and percussive movement is seen in such shows as the Australian *Tap Dogs*, and in the film *Bootmen*, a macho show where steel-capped boots strike metal bins and other parts of the set with great timing and skill.

British companies which show the roots of the jazz legacy are the Jiving Lindy-Hoppers and Zoots and Spangles, where performances include displays of the African influenced social dances of the 1940s and 50s like the *jitterbug* and the *jive*. Their style includes acrobatic partner work and jazzy steps in a typical relaxed, fluid style.

The music industry has manufactured many stars and dance styles which are for performance and participation. Disco dancing in its many forms has taken on a performance status of its own. It is a very competitive form with large networks of events. People like Madonna and her association with the New York gay craze for *voguing* have influenced the style. In the past John Travolta and Michael Jackson have been the ones to follow. Other related styles imported across the Atlantic, along with their own designer fashions, are robotics, break-dancing, moon-walking and so on. They have all had their turn on the street, in the clubs and in competition. They have the street value of participation but the competitiveness often results in a shift of emphasis to performance and the more virtuosity the better! Hip hop is now a $5 billion industry since its birth in the New York ghettos of the 1970s. Despite its known connections to crime, social violence and misogyny it continues to fascinate many. Some relate to it as part of the ongoing struggle of the poor and the oppressed, through dance and music. An interesting opinion is that it:

> '. . . constitutes an amateur folk form, through which the participants mediate their life experiences and create a sense of identity . . . continuing the tradition of black dancing.'[3]

Others see it as a cynical commercial enterprise. It has certainly been embraced by society at many levels. Nowadays you can even take classes in it at local ballet schools. It's cool to be Billy Elliot too. Indeed ballet and break dance have many similarities (not the posture!) as in the emphasis on physical feats.

---

[3] *Strut Your Funky Stuff!* Julie Tolley and Ramsay Burt in *New Dance*, 26 Autumn 1983.

A more homegrown version of showy club dancing is *bhangra*. Rooted in an ancient Punjabi celebration dance which is driven by a large loud drumbeat it has a fast and energetic style. Asian youth music and culture are pushing the boundaries to blend ancient and modern movement, sounds and values. It is now not unusual to see the large Chinese communities all over the world performing their athletic lion or dragon dances in the streets to celebrate their new year. There is even a troupe of authentic Hawaiian hula dancers in Brighton, Sussex.

Social Dance

We must not forget the ever-so-British ballroom dancing popularised by the BBC's *Come Dancing* programme. This is another style where participation was a priority, although nowadays the main aim is often competition. In the 1920s famous dancers Vernon and Irene Castle danced the polite, refined foxtrot. This followed on from the waltz which had gripped Europe for a century in its hypnotic 3/4 rhythm. The technique of the ballroom's quickstep, foxtrot, waltzes and tangos became more and more rule-ridden and this, once social dancing of the upper classes, declined in popularity and became a much more specialised cult pursuit. The 1920s brought a decline in musical standards of the big bands and fewer large ballrooms in favour of smaller, more intimate night clubs as fashions changed, reflecting the breakdown of the old British class structures. The West End glitter and glamour now subdued, the dancers moved out from London to the suburbs where there was space in the palais of the various large towns and cities.

The outbreak of World War II brought clothes rationing and the flowing fabrics so essential to the curving, fluid movements of dance had to be replaced with net (which was non-rationed). This gave a look of the – now familiar – ornately sequinned and jewelled yards of nylon net, which detracted from the original simple flow of the actual steps.

The still popular folk-dance clubs are a nostalgic reminder of Britain's rich dance heritage, now largely lost. Some of the dances and songs were saved by the research of Cecil Sharp, founder of the English Folk Dance and Song Society.

In other parts of Europe ancient circle dances have been preserved and are still danced regularly as part of community celebrations. The steps are often simple and gently repetitive as they sweep everyone along into a higher plane of oneness with nature, each other and themselves. As such they hint at their pagan origins. They developed in pre-Christian times to celebrate births, deaths, marriages and today circle dance is undergoing a revival. Many small groups are bringing a re-birth to old ways and values, not at odds with New Age politics, green awareness and concerns. Many are creating new music and steps as well as traditional ones, bringing the ancient into the here and now.

Scottish dancing has survived too and, of all the forms, has retained a masculine identity for dance. The Scottish Highland sword dance or *fling* would have originally been to celebrate a victory in battle, perhaps danced on the shield or sword of an opponent. In the face of many misrepresentations dancing became wrongly associated with the effeminate. The performing of tippy-toe dancing from the 1800s through to the early 1900s classified dancers as either adored sylph or whimpish admirer. Only in the Scottish style did dancing on the toes remain a symbol of masculine strength, even in a skirt! The dance event at the Highland Games is just as masculine as tossing the caber. Of course the women dance too and there is a strong tradition of Scottish country dancing.

The other popular dance which reinforced male influence, but actually banned women until recently, was the *morris*. The high leaps and athleticism are supposed to encourage the fertility and health of the community. Morris dancing would historically have been performed in the spring, at a time when the corn starts to grow; styles differ from one morris side to another and between different parts of the country. In the north it is a town dance, using very elaborate costume and clogs. Clog dancing even crossed the Atlantic to the USA where, joining with other influences, it became known as *Appalachian clog dancing*. This has come full circle returning to the UK in the late twentieth century.

The pagan origins of morris give it its basic style. This has been influenced over the centuries by a number of social influences: the African Moors (*Moorish/morris*) came to Europe and, it is said, this gave rise to the traditional blacking of the face, but others think that the sooted faces indicate something older than Christianity. Many morris sides were lost in the time of the Industrial Revolution as isolated rural life declined. Other modifications to the morris over time have been a) the season: no longer linked to pagan festivals but performed at holiday times as dictated by industry and business; b) the costume: from whatever ribbons and bells etc could be afforded to elaborately designed everyday clothes, and c) nowadays morris sides arrive in their cars, not by foot! As in many male recreational activities, morris dancing is often an excuse for a few pints and perhaps a release from the stresses of the hectic pace of life in the twenty-first century.

A few female sides exist even though there is still some disapproval. It is a strong tradition adapting and surviving with the times and continuing to give many the simple pleasure of joining in with dance.

Although folk dance, with its simple steps and figures, was originally intended to be social dance accessible for all, it too has become more virtuosic for professional performance. There are many examples from all over the world. One such is a real cross-cultural story dating back 2000 years when the Greek traders sailed along the Mediterranean coast not only trading goods. They also brought their music, stories and dances. The dance *La Farandole* is based on the Greek myth of Theseus and his journey into the labyrinth to slay the monster, the Minotaur. This simple line dance makes weaving and spiral maze floor patterns and is still danced by people in France today at festivals. Professional troupes (see 1.10) have developed and they add highly acrobatic display to the original simple skipping. This is originally in a line formation leading and following one behind the other, unlike American style *line dance*. This social dance is popular worldwide. Dancers are in a line side-by-side, wearing cowboy costumes to Country and Western music.

In a different sphere which seems to be many worlds away from traditional British dancing is the long saga of clubs and discos, *rock 'n roll*, the *twist*, the *pogo* of punk, *reggae* and now the land of *house music* and *raves*. These temples of energetic endless dancing attract hundreds and thousands of people at a time. Most of it originated once again in the USA. The house music is relentless and often drug-assisted punters help maintain the tempo for hours. There is a massive financial profit to be made by the organisers but it is bringing back the simple pleasure of dance to many.

Another style of social dance which has achieved recent popularity in the 1990s is the Latin-American based *sambas*, *salsas* and *lambadas*, and the original type *tango*. Unlike raves these are dances for couples. There are many classes and social gatherings organised for these dances. There are schools of Samba where people can be in the samba band or the

1.10 *Li Gai Farandoulaire. The Farandole*

spectacular dance displays, reminiscent of Brazil's *Mardi Gras*. They also teach the dances to keen onlookers. Evenings end with everyone dancing together.

The world in the twenty-first century is a melting pot of different cultures and possibly one of the most exotic is Egyptian dance. It is mostly performed by females, with its origins being traceable as far back as 5,500 BC in female dominated societies of the Middle East. The female body was worshipped for its ability to bear children. It is one of the most ancient dances known. Its symbolic attachment to female fertility and healthy childbirth now inspires many women. As a sophisticated dance technique its simple steps and graceful flow are enjoyed by many. This is a dance form which crosses the boundary as a form of fitness training too, which we will cover in the following section.

THE FITNESS FACTOR

Although not strictly speaking dance, these fitness activities are often used by dancers in training.

---

[4] http://li.gai.farandoulaire.free.fr

'Working out' is now one of the most common kinds of exercise methods, but contrary to popular belief, it *did* exist pre-Fonda. Movement exercise to music has been popular since the 1930s. Later 'aerobics', in various forms, boomed and is developing in many ways. This includes callanetics, step-classes, stretch n'tone, low-impact, high-impact and even competitions. As the exercises are performed the heart rate rises and so muscles are toned and the heart itself strengthened.

A wide variety of body conditioning activities with and without weights and/or machines are available. *Pilates* is one such method developed in the 1930s. It strengthens and conditions the body through a series of exercises performed in a balanced sequence. There is a good deal of attention to working isolated muscle groups through natural movements, often with machine assistance. It also encourages better posture.

The *Feldenkrais Method* is based on over 40 years research by Dr Moshe Feldenkrais. It uses gentle movement suitable for all ages and abilities and emphasises learning more intelligent ways of moving, so that stresses, aches and pains are reduced. Another such approach is the *Alexander Technique* which releases tension and teaches us how to use our bodies more efficiently. This inner focus as a way of working owes much to the influence of Eastern philosophy. Yoga, tai'chi, shiatsu, massage and various healing techniques are available now more than ever. They are the New Age aerobics if you like!

Yoga is probably the best known and most popular technique. The word *yoga* means 'union' and it sets out to unify the mind, body and spirit in harmony with the universe. It exercises everything from internal organs to the hair on your head. Movement is slow with prolonged stillnesses emphasising breathing, stretching, relaxation, diet and positive thought through meditation. It is an ancient Hindu discipline dating back before it was written down in 300 BC.

Tai'chi and aikido both originate from the Far East and are gentle martial arts. They concentrate on meditation, relaxation, balance, flexibility and co-ordination. They are non-violent and aim to develop sensitive contact and control. Since the earliest classical period of Chinese medicine exercises to strengthen the constitution, enhance vitality and ensure good health have been a central part of the healing tradition. Influenced at different times by Taoist and Buddhist philosophies, by the theories of self-defence, the study of animal movement and natural science as much as by medical theories alone, these exercises belong to a rich traditional heritage. There are many different forms but all of them have in common a few central principles. These concern posture, breathing and mental concentration or visualisation and they are all concerned with promoting the subtle energy in the body which the Chinese call *chi*. The chi flows through a network of channels which connect internal organs with the rest of the body and help us to function harmoniously. Many forms of alternative medicine like acupuncture, reflexology and shiatsu are now easily available.

So if we reflect on the fitness factor in Britain we see an interesting East-West divide. The hi-energy, body-beautiful politics from the United States contrasts with the gentler, more meditative approach of the East. This more holistic (*treat the person as a whole*), inside-out approach is often known as 'alternative'. You pays your money and you takes your choice!

DANCE TRAINING

At present you are probably studying dance at school or college. You may be considering taking your dance education further and are wondering where you may be able to do so. There are lots of choices as the world of dance becomes more organised. No longer is the path one of local dancing school, then stage school or if you are lucky (and the correct height and weight) the Royal Ballet School. Neither is it true that you have to be young to train. Nowadays there are many different options other than performing. There is work in therapy, in notation, teaching, dance administration or research.

The chances to join in dance classes are many, whether in local studios, youth dance groups, community centres or summer schools. These all build towards increasing levels of technical and choreographic skills, so that when applying for full-time training you have prepared yourself adequately. Moving on to full-time training there are many fine colleges and schools in existence. The Laban Centre, London Contemporary Dance School and the Rambert School are such places and are all of a very high standard, but the fees are high too. Universities also offer dance courses of a very high calibre and a degree at the end. MAs and PhDs are now more and more common too. There is also a range of courses for those who wish to go into teaching in schools or in the community.

Other avenues of training are in the aerobics and fitness areas. Often these involve working on short courses, or in the more holistic styles it can involve close association with an expert in that particular field.

So you can see in the world of dance nowadays there are many choices. There is still the traditional route into performing with a ballet company or in West End shows, pop videos, nightclubs and television.

REFERENCES

Further Reading

Magazines

Dance Now from www.dancebooks.co.uk
Dance Theatre journal (quarterly), Laban Centre, www.laban.org
Dancing Times (monthly), www.dancing-times.co.uk

Books

Anderson, Jack (1974) *Dance*, Newsweek Books.
Beaumont, Cyril W. (1981) *Michel Fokine and His Ballets*, Princeton Book Co.
Bremner, Martha (ed.) (1999) *Fifty Contemporary Choreographers*, Routledge.
Clarke, Mary and Crisp, Clement (1978) *Ballet: An Illustrated History*, A&C Black. (1989) *London Contemporary Dance Theatre, The First Twenty-one Years*, Dance Books. (1981) *The History of Dance*, Random House.
Craine, Debra and Mackrell, Judith (2000) *The Oxford Dictionary of Dance*, Oxford University Press.
Ellfeldt, Lois (1976) *Dance from Magic to Art*, WCB.
Jordan, Stephanie (1992) *Striding Out: Aspects of Contemporary and New Dance in Britain*. Dance Books.
Mackrell, Judith (1992) *Out of Line: The Story of British New Dance*, Dance Books.
Pritchard, Jane (1997) *Rambert A Celebration. A Survey of the First 70 years*, Rambert Dance Company.
Quirey, Belinda (2002) *May I Have the Pleasure? The Story of Popular Dancing*, Dance Books.
Stearns, Marshall and Jean (1993) *Jazz Dance: The Story of American Vernacular Dance*, Da Capo Press.

Video and DVD

From the National Resource Centre for Dance: www.surrey.ac.uk/NRCD
Coming Home, Adzido Pan African Dance Co. *The House of Bones and*

Different Dancers Similar Motion, Motionhouse. *Soda Lake*, Richard Alston. *Façade*, Frederick Ashton.

From Dance Books www.dancebooks.co.uk *Ballet Rambert, Different Steps*. Shows *Sgt. Early's Dream, Death and the Maiden*. *Five dances by Martha Graham*, Martha Graham Dance Company. *La Fille mal Gardée*, Frederick Ashton, Royal Ballet, recorded 1981. *Les Sylphides*, on *The Glory of the Bolshoi*, rec. 1991. *Paris dances Diaghilev*, includes *Petrushka, Faune, Les Noces*, rec. 1991. *The Firebird and Les Noces*, Royal Ballet, rec. 2001. *The Prince of the Pagodas*, Kenneth Macmillan. *The Sleeping Beauty*, Kirov Ballet, rec. 1992.

From Dancing Times www.dancing-times.co.uk *Explosive Dance*. A mix of ballet, lindy hop, salsa, flamenco and Riverdance. *Changing Steps*. Merce Cunningham.

From The Video Place www.theplace.org.uk On the Spring Re-Loaded series; *Out of Here*, Candoco.

From www.greencandle.com *Tales from the Citadel*, Green Candle.

From: enquiries@edresources.co.nz Ihi FrENZy video resource pack (New Zealand Ministry of Education)

Web sites

www.adzido.co.uk
www. merce.org – Merce Cunningham
www.shobanajeyasingh.co.uk
www.theplace.org.uk – Richard Alston Dance Company
www.nzballet.org.nz

Chapter 2

THE SKILL OF DANCE

A STARTING POINT – DANCE TECHNIQUE

As your body matures it will require new challenges in dance. Technical training is demanding, especially at first, but it is also fun. In a dance class the harder you work, the more you will build up skills and confidence.

The aims of technical training in dance are to:

- make the body more mobile;

- strengthen the body;

- develop awareness of the body centre;

- develop co-ordination;

- widen your awareness of movement possibilities;

- help to develop confidence in your own body.

The dancer's body is an instrument. Like a piano, it must be tuned, but this is only the start. Technique alone is not enough, it needs to be combined with imagination in order to create dances. This cocktail of technique and imagination will stimulate new ideas for moving which are appropriate to whatever you may wish to express. Eventually you will be able to compose dances which reveal your own special style.

Some dancers have created their own styles of technique and choreography. These styles are physically demanding and in schools a 'softer' technique is more appropriate. This is reflected in dance exercises. Exercises are designed to assist the young dancer to move safely, correctly, confidently, with a sense of enjoyment and freedom.

2.1 Martha Graham in IMPERIAL GESTURE *(1935)*

GOOD STUDIO PRACTICE

'The mind is a muscle'
Yvonne Rainer[1]

On a simple physical level the class starts usually with a series of safe warm-up exercises to release tensions and prepare the muscles and the mind.

Vulnerable areas of the body such as the back, shoulders, neck, hips, knees, ankles and feet should be carefully warmed, relaxed and

---

[1] Yvonne Rainer, *The Vision of Modern Dance* (1979), ed. Jean Morrison Brown, Dance Books, p. 141. This was the title of a dance and an account of her work, written in 1965 and published in 1975.

2.2 *Graham's unique use of the spine in contractions and release. London Contemporary Dance Theatre in Residency at I. M. Marsh College, Liverpool (1974)*

extended. You should try to feel that you are 'getting into' your body, like trying on some new clothes. There should also be some thought given to how the skeleton and muscles work and how breathing affects the flow of energy.

EXERCISE 1: a combination exercise to use for warming up.
Start with the feet shoulder width apart, arms raised above the head.

a. Step in place 4 times and each time stretch up through the ribs and on throughout the fingertips.

b. **CHECK** that as you step you go through the whole foot smoothly – toe, ball, heel – and that your arms stay above your head. **STRETCH AS FAR AS YOU CAN.**

c. Bring the feet closer (under the hip bones) drop the arms and feel the abdominal muscles pull up. Breathing in, roll down, head leading to *d*; bend your knees as you do this. You should feel a comfortable stretch in your back. Breathe out and stretch the legs dropping the head and keeping your weight forwards. Feel a stretch through the hamstrings *e*. Do not worry if you cannot keep your hands on the floor, try to stretch without too much strain. Now roll up with bent knees that gradually straighten. When standing start again. Repeat 4 times.

This exercise stretches the feet, legs, back and it strengthens the abdominal muscles. Try to breathe deeply all the time and allow the stretch to deepen into the joints.

EXERCISE 2: a good swing exercise to mobilise your waist.
a. Stand in parallel (feet under hips), arms to side.
b. Swing your arms side to side wrapping them around the body and opening them each time.

You can also do this stepping with the direction of the swing and you can allow the momentum of the swing to take you into a 3 step turn sideways. It is fun to experiment with what else the swing can take you into.

a)   b)

Exercises such as slow shoulder rotations, overhead arm stretches, rolling down and up, from standing, and careful trudging on the spot are a few useful ones.

A warm-up should include exercises which intensify gradually. First some gentle aerobic work, then some safe stretching. Usually it takes around fifteen minutes to raise the body temperature sufficiently, although on colder days this may take longer. At this point you may have worked up a light sweat.

The effects of warm-up are:

- warms your muscles to improve flexibility and strength;
- increases heart and breathing rates;
- increases blood flow to muscles bringing more oxygen;
- improves speed of reflexes.

These are all important to help you avoid injury. They also warm up your mind so that you are better co-ordinated and more alert.

THE SKILL OF DANCE

More demanding stretches and exercises should now be introduced for strengthening of the abdominal muscles, the backs and the legs, as well as more energetic swings, more demanding extensions and sequences.

Repetition of sequences improves your co-ordination and movement memory.

At the end of an energetic class you should cool down for about ten minutes. This allows your body to keep the blood flowing and remove waste products, which have built up in the muscles, from the body. One of these is *lactic acid*, and it is this which causes you to feel stiff if it is allowed to pool in the muscles. In your cool-down you should sit or lie down to stretch the big muscle groups such as torso, legs (hamstrings, calves, quadriceps) and shoulders. You can also walk to cool down.

Task 1

- After a class make a list of as many exercises as you can remember. Describe what each one is for. Use counts and diagrams if it is helpful.

Discuss.

- How do you feel at the end of a technique class?
- What has happened to you?

CENTERING

'That little magnet in the centre that holds you together'

Hanya Holm[2]

After a number of technique classes you may detect a difference in the way you feel. One of the most obvious ways in which you may notice a change is in your posture. Good posture is vital for control, safety and expression. We say that the body is correctly **aligned**, ie it forms a straight line from head to feet. There should be a feeling of freedom, easy movement, effortless carriage of the head and an awareness of energy

---

[2] Hanya Holm, *Vision of Modern Dance*, p. 74.

travelling out in all directions from the centre to all body parts. In this way you can 'move away' from your centre while still retaining your poise and balance.

One of the causes of poor alignment is the blocking effect of tension, eg lifted or rounded shoulders or sticking the hips out backwards. The exercises at the start of class should help you to learn how to relax muscles when they are not needed. Correct use of the various muscle groups is the only way to bring the skeleton into alignment. In this way you will become more balanced and be able to move efficiently and expressively.

Task 2

Carry this out in pairs, one checking, one moving. Stand still. Check:

- Feet parallel – line them up under the hips. Check that the insides of the heel and big toe are in a straight line.
- Lift the arches of the feet so that the weight of the body is distributed under the heel, big toe and outside front edge of the foot, and evenly on both feet.
- Thighs slightly lifted to support hips.
- Energise and lift abdominal muscles, drop tail bone. Feel the back wide and supporting the arms.
- Lengthen the neck, let the head float, drop the shoulders.
- Tighten buttocks.
- Breathe in 'through the soles of the feet' and let the breath flow up through the body opening, filling and softening all the joints.
- Breathe out through the top of the head.

Do Not:

- Lift shoulders
- Hold breath
- Drop/lift chin
- Tuck hips under
- Tilt them forwards.
- **Now** feel this position and rise easily onto a half-toe. Swing arms easily and move head without loss of balance. Use your bones for support and feel control from your centre outwards into space.

- **You may try this either with legs parallel or turned out. Both positions require you to connect heels to the tops of your legs so that control of the legs always uses the large upper leg muscles, rather than the more vulnerable knees and ankles.**

Good alignment is not still; it is a dynamic readiness for movement. Watch when someone starts to walk – the body tilts forward. As they walk the 'plumb line' remains. Energy is wasted if sections of the body need to be corrected and pulled into line. In order to balance, the muscle groups must be stretched and strengthened to increase:

1. **Flexibility:** the range of movement in the joints which is increased by lengthening the muscle fibres. Stretching in held relaxed positions avoids muscle damage. Bouncing stretches, such as bouncing to touch toes, are unsafe because they tend to tear muscles and other soft tissue around the joints like ligaments and tendons.
2. **Strength:** the amount of force a muscle can apply against resistance, eg. a weight, which is developed by increasing repetitions of movement or the use of weight on a muscle during exercise.

Another essential skill which your body needs to avoid injury is **stamina.** Muscles can keep 'going', as in continuous jumping, only for so long before they tire, this is stamina. You may have experienced the pounding heart, fast breathing and burning in your quadriceps after a long travelling and jumping sequence in your dance class. You will have reached a point of fatigue and your muscles are telling you to rest. When tiredness sets in your body is vulnerable to mistakes and injury. Therefore, it is important to build up stamina of heart, lungs and muscles, so that you can dance for longer safely. Aerobic activities, such as jogging, cycling and swimming help to build stamina. So, if you don't already, why not start cycling to school?

Once you begin to feel a sense of central control, moving and co-ordination will be easier. Trained dancers appear to move easily, confidently and expressively on stage because they have built an instinctive sense of alignment from their centre. Centering is both physical and psychological. It refers to *a*) the centre of weight of a body and *b*) feeling whole and grounded **IN** the body.

The centre of gravity is the most dense portion in the body, in the pelvis slightly below the navel. Being 'centred' operates as a feeling of correctness and ease, a oneness with motion. When moving correctly, it increases the dancer's ability to express the sense of the dance through the accuracy of movement and the projection of the meaning to the audience.

SAFE PERSONAL PRACTICE

'Injuries can happen because dance is a high risk business'
Peter Brinson and Fiona Dick[3]

So far in this chapter there has been advice on how to prevent injury, for example by proper warm-up. However, no matter how hard we try sometimes injuries can still happen. Practical things that you can do to further avoid injury are:

- Wear layers of clothing which can be peeled off and replaced when necessary.

- Do not dance if you have an injury, a fever, or after a heavy meal.

- Try to work on suitably sprung floors which are clean, smooth and non-slip.

- A suitable room temperature is recognised as between 18° to 24°C.

- Do not smoke.

If you have a muscle or joint injury you should know how to treat it so that it has a chance to heal quickly and thoroughly. An easy to remember first-aid formula is:

Rest – Ice – Compress – Elevate. Spells **RICE**.

When you first have an injury ice it. A support bandage may need to be used to compress the site. Once the worst swelling has gone down alternating heat and cold for a few days helps, as does rest and keeping

---

[3] In *Fit to Dance?* (1996), Calouste Gulbenkian Foundation (UK), p. 14.

the injury raised to take off the weight. If an injury persists you may need to see your doctor and if it keeps recurring a visit to a physiotherapist or some compensatory exercises may be needed.

Finally, proper nutrition helps to prevent injury. Research shows[4] that dancers eat too much fat and not enough carbohydrate.

A balanced diet may look like this:

- Fruit and vegetables (vitamins) – 33%

- Rice, bread, pasta, potatoes (carbohydrates) – 32%

- Dairy (for bones, teeth, energy) – 15%

- Meat, fish, eggs, pulses (proteins) – 12%

- Fats/sugar – 8%

- Water – for all body processes the body needs 2 to 3 litres a day. Sweet sticky drinks and too much tea or coffee are not a substitute for water and can be harmful.

If you kept a food diary for a week, how would it add up?

We are bombarded, by the media and fashion world, with the idea that 'thin is in'. It is easy to be brain washed by this. Dancers can be prone to eating disorders such as *bulimia* (binge eating) and *anorexia nervosa* (self-starvation) in foolish attempts to achieve a sylph image. Try to remember you are what you eat and to stay healthy you must eat healthily.

ACTION TIME!

'Your training gives you freedom'

Martha Graham[5]

The joints of your body are capable of only three basic actions:

- FLEXION (bending)

- EXTENSION (stretching)

- ROTATION (turning).

---

[4] Ibid, p. 148.
[5] In *Prime Movers* (1977), Joseph H. Mazo, A & C Black Ltd, p. 157.

It is interesting to note that the skeleton and muscles of the body function as a simple machine. For example whenever a part of the body bends (flexes), the corresponding side of that part will stretch (extend). So if you bend your arm the biceps flexes while the triceps stretches. Joints also rotate: try this with your shoulders, ankles, ribs and hips. Hip rotations are noticeable in such techniques as jazz dance or African dance. The richness of dance arises from the many combinations of these simple functions. In the *Martha Graham* style of modern dance when a contraction appears the abdominals flex and the back muscles stretch, giving the torso a characteristic curved appearance. Similarly in the *Cunningham* style there is an interest in the upper, middle and lower sections of the spine curving independently as well as together. This gives the spine a more vertical stance akin to that of classical ballet, but with more possibilities of mobility. In both styles the spine functions as a separate limb.

More recently, *Release Techniques* of New Dance focus on how the body moves anatomically in a series of small, slow, gentle movements. The aim is to awaken understanding of how muscles, joints and organs actually work. Such systems as the *Alexander Technique* and *Feldenkrais* fall into this category. Both of these approaches concentrate on how movement *feels* rather than its outward appearance. The following exercise is an example:

> *Standing easily, concentrate on breathing, imagining it filling and emptying the body. See it as light which brightens the rooms of your body and see the ribs and diaphragm muscle increasing the space for air as you inhale. As you exhale the space decreases. Take 10 minutes or so to do this and so feel how breath works and how it can help movement to be both safer and more adventurous. It may even encourage you to yawn! Sounds wonderful!*

Task 3

In pairs, try the three basic actions (flex, extend, rotate) while sitting, kneeling, standing and lying down, using fingers, toes, ankles, shoulders, elbows, hips etc. Always try to connect the body parts to your centre and isolate the part so that it is the only part moving. Make a simple phrase which you can dance, mirroring your partner.

These isolated gestures can feel and look quirky, but when they are combined endless numbers of complicated actions result.

THE SIX DANCE ACTIONS

After warming up the class concentrates on more complex combinations of movements, which are combinations of the six following Dance Actions:

1. TRAVELLING

2. JUMPING

3. TURNING

4. GESTURE

5. STILLNESS

6. FALLING

1. Travelling

This consists of basic stepping patterns as well as others such as rolling, sliding and crawling. Singly or in combination they can make interesting rhythms and spatial patterns. Some basic step patterns are listed below.

- **Walk** – even rhythm. In a natural walk the heel goes to the floor first. Sometimes a walk is stylised so that the toes touch first. Pull up the centre to keep smooth control and alignment.

- **Run** – a fast walk needing more foot and leg extension.

- **Prance** – a run with a lift of the knees. Requires strong foot extension so that the free knee lifts up sharply.

- **Triplet** – a stylised walk in a 3/4 rhythm. Smooth, waltz-like. Merce Cunningham once remarked that when humans invented the waltz they must have felt like they needed three feet. Why do you think this is?

Other patterns include:

Skip (hop, step)
Slide (glide step, cut step)
Gallop (step, cut step)
Polka (hop step, step, draw step)
Schottische (step, draw step, step, hop)
Mazurka (glide step, cut step, hop).

All of the above usually hold the arms or let them swing freely in opposition to the legs for balance.

Task 4

1. Try triplets very slowly and gradually accelerate until they become running, feel the contrast in speed.
2. Change a walk from being light, free and continuous to strong and interrupted, feel the contrast in flow and dynamics.

What might these changes express to an onlooker?

Stepping patterns form a rich range of movement for folk and social dances. Country dances were based on simple steps: runs, walks, skips, hops and so on.

Social dancing has often been used by well-known choreographers. Frederick Ashton's *Façade* starts with a Highland fling and later a polka is danced by a woman who rips her skirt to perform wildly in her bloomers! The work also features a charleston danced by two flappers, four girls waltzing and a mock-passionate tango.

Similarly in his ballet *La Fille Mal Gardée (The Unchaperoned Daughter)* there is clogging, maypole and morris dancing. Christopher Bruce, the choreographer of *Sergeant Early's Dream*, uses folk-influenced steps and music. He makes up his own folky steps using influences from tap dance and Irish step dancing mixed with a contemporary style which involves a contracted torso and flexed feet and hands. This is similar to the style of Martha Graham. His dances are often concerned with the lives of communities so the folk influence is very appropriate.

Matthew Bourne often uses social dance steps and styles. In his *Swan Lake* (1995) the ball scene uses various social dances. He elaborates on

2.3 'The Tango' from FAÇADE *(1931) choreography Frederick Ashton. Dancers Margot Fonteyn and Robert Helpmann*

the steps and rhythms of waltz, tango, flamenco, tarantella, adding balletic style lifts and even at one point making a fun kind of conga line.

Other choreographers include travelling on the hands or rolling across the floor. In Christopher Bruce's *Ghost Dances* the ghosts are evil creatures, they slither, roll and slide almost like snakes. In the dance *Flesh and Blood* (1989) by Lea Anderson for The Cholmondeleys, the dancers crawl and roll to make a scene full of wriggling bodies. These are lowly creatures, insects and reptiles, and because *Flesh and Blood* links to religious themes we may interpret this travelling to be associated with suffering in hell. For those of you who are not familiar with the mediaeval painting *Hell* by Hieronymous Bosch, or the twentieth century graphics of M.C. Escher, it would be worth researching into these images which may have influenced Anderson's choreography.

2.4 DANCESCAPES *(1979), choreography Linda Ashley. Dancers Sally-Ann Connor and Diana Brightling*

2. Jumping

Human movements have preparation, action and recovery phases. This is particularly important in safe jumping.

Task 5

In pairs, go through the sequence below slowly and continuously three times:

- Bend knees (lift abdominal muscles) – **PREPARATION**
- Extend feet and stretch legs to rise – **ACTION**

- Lower through toe, ball, heel of feet
- Bend knees – **RECOVERY**.

At all times breathe evenly and hold arms by your sides. Where is your focus?

Now repeat it but faster and more suddenly so that it becomes a bouncy jump. **Every landing is a take-off.**

Check that your partner goes through the heel on each landing and stretches legs and feet in the air. Also check the alignment of their torso; are they maintaining a plumb line? Are their knees and feet aligned?

The five types of jumps

- HOP – take-off and land on the same foot;
- LEAP – take-off one foot, land on the other foot;
- JUMP – take-off two feet, land on two feet;
  take-off two feet, land on one foot;
  take-off one foot, land on two feet.

Task 6

1. Do one of the five jumps continuously.
2. Combine it with two others to make a phrase of steps and jumps.

Jumping is an exciting part of dance. In Robert North's *Troy Game* the dancers jump exhaustively. One section, a mock fight for two men, is even performed all on one leg, mostly hopping while using the arms and other leg to gesture. The height of their leaps is breathtaking.

Your aim, as your jumping skills improve, should be to feel a moment when you are suspended in the air, yet still land safely. You can experiment with jumps to falls, turning jumps, different leg gestures and different shapes in the air.

3. Turning

There are many types of turn; varying degrees (ie full, less or more); inward and outward; on and off-balance; while jumping, sitting or lying; spinning or pivoting and so on.

2.5 TROY GAME *(1974), choreography Robert North, London Contemporary Dance Theatre*

All these require good placement and a strong sense of centre to avoid loss of balance. It helps if your eyes focus on where you are headed. 'Spotting', used extensively in ballet, is useful but not essential. Spotting is fixing the eyes on a point for as long as possible then whipping the head round as quickly as possible to see the point again. It helps to avoid dizziness, but it gives a specific look which may not be appropriate to your choreography.

Turns can start from rising onto a half-toe, or by throwing or swinging a limb, and they can be performed on various parts of the body; knees, hips, front of the body, hands, feet etc. Turns make you feel as if your universe is turning around you, and are challenging to perform.

In many classic Indian dance styles the turns are an important element. In *Kathak*, from North India and Pakistan, the *chukras* are exciting whipped turns. In *Bharatha Natyam* a turn often symbolises a change of character from the Hindu religious myths. The dancer literally turns from god Krishna into goddess Radha. Multiple turns and spins are characteristic of ballet and break dancing.

4. Gesture

Gestures are movements of parts of the body which do not involve supporting weight. The language of gesture is rich and endless.

Robert Cohan's *Waterless Method of Swimming Instruction* contains a humorous section where the men use arm gestures to convey the idea of paddling a boat, and hip rotations to add the feel of a playful Latin samba.

Nowhere is gesture used in a more detailed way than in the mudras of the southern Indian *Kathakali* dance-drama. The hands tell a story and seem to take on a life of their own, reinforced by subtle, powerful facial gestures.

African dance uses gesture too. In the Waloof tradition, from Senegal, there is a difficult 'circling' of the legs. The Zulu Warrior Dance uses high leg kicking gestures.

Classical ballet uses mime gestures to tell the story or to draw characters. In the ballet *Petrouchka* (1911) by Michel Fokine, the puppet's gestures are stiff and wooden distinguishing him from the human characters.

Building on a classical ballet story Matthew Bourne's modern dance *Swan Lake* changes the villagers into a cast from the 1950s and 60s social dance scene celebrating the young prince's coming of age. He uses the twitchy isolated shoulder, hip and hand gestures of the jitterbug, the twist and the shake. Also he uses the famous Elvis pelvic thrust gesture to add a sexual and provocative edge to the young prince's riotous night.

Task 7

Find a painting by Miro or Paul Klee. Using as many different parts of your body as possible, trace the images. Combine gestures both on the spot and travelling. Use different dynamics to suggest the shapes, colours and textures.

The dance of Lea Anderson often uses gesture, as in the videodance *Cross Channel* (1991). The cyclists use head gestures in the section seated on a park bench reading, and when lying in the grass, flyswotting. Later the head and hand gestures are emphasised by burying the rest of the body in the sand.

5. Stillness

Being still is being active!

Silence in music, space in painting, stillness in dance are all essential to clear expression. In dance stillness often involves balance requiring total control. Stillness can be held on different parts of the body. In order to control a balance on one foot try the following: push down into the floor through the standing foot; feel your centre pulling up away through the abdominal muscles; feel energy flowing outwards away from your centre to your limbs and back to the centre; hold the stillness. Ensure that your hips and knees are always lined up with the middle of your feet whether in parallel, turn-out or turned in.

Dances often start and end with stillness, so it is important to have control over balance and a feel for keeping energy alive in the body even when still.

Stillness is used frequently in Richard Alston's *Soda Lake* (1981). This dance is based around images of a vast desert landscape in North America and the sculptures by Nigel Hall on the same theme which are the stage set. The whole motionless scene gives rise to several distinctive still body shapes; the 'sentinel position' a low lying position with an outward watching expression; and the 'big bird', a high one leg balance resembling a hovering vulture.

In Mark Morris's *The Hard Nut* (1991) as based on the story of the *Nutcracker*, stillness is used during the transformation scene. The *Nutcracker* character cracks the nut, breaking the curse on the ugly princess, and she becomes beautiful. It is a real twilight zone moment as the dancers hold stillness as if time stands still. In the background a whirly time vortex swirls and all adds to the magical transformation.

6. Falling

There are two different types of falls:

- an off-balance fall;

- a collapse.

Loss of balance will make you fall. Doris Humphrey built a dance technique on the belief that dance occurs in the frightening moment between falling and recovery. As the body shifts its weight it either gives into, or resists, the pull of gravity and this is felt and sensed expressively.

When you fall it is an intentional 'giving-in' to gravity, but your centre pulls you up and this co-ordination helps to avoid injury. If recovery is instant you will rebound. Avoid landing on knees, elbows, tip of shoulder, hands or tailbone . . . there should be a smooth, successive placing of your body to the floor. Improving your dance technique is one of the best ways of learning how to move correctly and therefore, avoid injury.

A rebounding fall was used in Adzido Pan African Dance Ensemble's *Under African Skies* (1990). It examines the tragedies of apartheid as symbolised by an arrogant armed soldier. The dancers react with sudden, heavy falls but immediately they bounce up with defiant, challenging cries of protest for freedom.

A collapse tends to drop suddenly through your centre of gravity and not rebound up.

Lloyd Newson's style of dance for DV8 often involves repeated falls. The dancers hurl themselves at each other, falling and catching frantically. They sometimes seem to be lovers but at other times in deadly combat. This type of dangerous, demanding work requires strength, stamina and co-ordination which should be included in the dancers' training to help prevent injury.

Task 8

Write the six Dance Actions and the numbers 1 to 6 on separate pieces of paper. Close your eyes and pick each piece of paper out in turn and make a phrase in the order that you chose them, ie five jumps followed by two turns etc.

Making dances from individual dance steps in this chance process is a useful starting point if you are stuck for ideas.

Through dance technique we learn to manage our bodies efficiently and safely, whilst also meeting new challenges. The centred, flexible, strong body can continue the six actions just mentioned in endless ways – the only limit is your imagination.

Your teacher may have taught you a set study by now. Try to pinpoint which actions it uses. Which ones do you find more difficult? Is this because you lose your balance? Which muscles can help you improve your performance? Or perhaps your feet are not working correctly. Try to pinpoint your weaknesses so that you can work to improve them.

Task 9

Choose a phrase or section of a set study and add your own ideas to it. Improvise to find actions which are similar in style and feel to the original.

EXPRESSIVE SKILLS

As your physical skill levels start to improve you may be preparing for a performance. This needs another layer of expressive skills and these are:

- **Focus** – A dancer needs to maintain total concentration and involvement when performing. No talking, fidgeting, playing with hair or pulling down those wedgies! Well, unless that is part of the dance.

Focus can differ in terms of where, when and how, depending on what needs to be expressed. Some dances need the traditional strong focus, thrown out and up to the back row of the audience. Other dances may need focus to be softer, more introvert and inward as in the character Petrouchka in the Fokine ballet, or held on a fixed point in space as in Christopher Bruce's *Sergeant Early's Dream*. The dancers, immigrants a long way from home, gaze out to the backdrop, a seascape, and beyond the horizon to their homeland. The use of eyes and focus is very important in South Asian dance. A Bharatha Natyam dancer can show the look of wonder on Krishna's mother's face when she catches him

2.6 *THE MAD BAD LINE (1990) choreography Linda Ashley for BAD Dance Co. Notice the varied use of focus*

eating mud and on ordering him to open his mouth she sees the entire heavens inside.

Lea Anderson's characteristic use of facial gestures exploits to the full the expressive potential of focus.

> 'Eyes close and then open to reveal pupils fixed in an upward gaze, as if looking towards life after death and its rewards ... In *Flesh and Blood* the dancer's emotions are arrested and harnessed in movement ...'
>
> *Sophie Constanti*[6]

- **Projection** – Similarly to focus, this enhances the expression of the ideas behind the dance to the audience. Projection throws out energy giving life to the movement. The pioneer modern dancer of the start of the twentieth century, Isadora Duncan, believed that

[6] *First and Last*, in '*Dancing Times*', January 1990.

energy could travel across space to touch the audience's feelings. Correct breathing helps control the projection of energy. It can be powerful or more understated, as would be perhaps appropriate to some post modern dance using a softer *Release* style.

Indian classical dancers of Kathak style are highly trained in the projection of energy outwards from the centre to the finger tips and eyes. In an exploration of this Akram Khan's *Fix* (2000) plays with the direction of energy. In a fusion of Kathak and modern genres he projects the energy out and pulls it back into the centre.

- **Interpretation** – A dancer needs to be sensitive in interpreting and being able to express the content, themes or roles of a dance. Different dancers will dance the same role in their own way with subtle variations of phrasing, timing and dynamics. Here we read praise of the performance of Vaslav Nijinsky in the leading role of the ballet *Petrouchka*, in 1911 and how this differed from the choreographer Fokine's own interpretation:

'He is a puppet and – remarkable touch – a puppet with a soul . . . his facial expression never changes; yet the pathos is greater, more keenly carried across the footlights, than one could imagine possible . . . I have seen Fokine in the same role, and although he gives you all the gestures the result is not the same. Who can ever forget Nijinsky . . . rushing about waving his pathetically stiff arms in the air, and finally beating his way with his clenched fists through the paper window to curse the stars? It is a more poignant expression of grief than most Romeos can give us.'

Carl van Vechten[7]

It seems that the dancer Nijinsky interpreted the role more expressively than the choreographer himself.

- **Musicality** – A dancer needs a sense of rhythm and musical structure which runs through the whole body, not just the ears. This may involve responding to certain instruments, or changes in tempo and being able to keep to a time signature such as a waltz in 3/4 time.

[7] In *Balanchine's Complete Stories or the Great Ballets* (1954). Ed. Francis Mason, Doubleday & Co. Inc., p. 275.

2.7 NINE SONGS (1993) Cloud Gate Dance Theatre of Taiwan, choreographer Lin Hwai-min, dancer Li Wen-long. Focus, projection and expression are clear even in a still photograph

Of course being able to count in time and remember the correct movements for those counts is bread and butter to a dancer. 'Dancer's counts' are helpful here. This is the method of counting but starting each bar with its number as in:

3/4 123 223 323 423

this is 4 bars of waltz time. The use of the bar numbers helps the motor memory.

Even so there are some choreographers who expect dancers to relate to music differently. For example in Merce Cunningham's work, sometimes the dancers have never heard the music before the opening night and it may be ear splitting. However, the dancer's own counts are so well-rehearsed that they can dance accurately to the rhythms as set in rehearsal.

Overall these performance skills are often built up during rehearsal as choreographer and dancer communicate to make and shape a dance. It is a team effort to ensure that the choreographer's intention is expressed and communicated to the audience. Chapter 8 deals with rehearsal process in more detail.

Further Reading

Cerry, Sandra (1989) *Body and Self: Partners in Movement*, Minton, Human Kinetic Publishers Inc.

Frich, Elizabeth (1983) *Matt Mattox Book of Jazz Dance*, Sterling Publishing.

Howse, J. (1992) *Dance Technique and Injury Prevention*, A & C Black.

Sherborn, Elizabeth (1975) *On the Count of One*, Mayfield Publishing Co.

Videos and DVD

From www.dancebooks.co.uk *Swan Lake*, Matthew Bourne and Adventures in Motion Pictures; *The Hard Nut*, Mark Morris.

From *Dancing Times Magazine* – www.dancing-times.co.uk *Enter Achilles*, DV8; *Ghost Dances*, Christopher Bruce, Houston Ballet.

From The Video Place www.theplace.org.uk *Fix*, Akram Khan on *Spring Re-Loaded 6*.

Music

Available from www.ucamusic.com For travelling, stepping and jumping: *Plus Ten* and *Fast Rock*, on *Springsound*, Michelle Scullion, 2002 Melectra Music. *Mare's Wedding* (Radha Sahar) and *Paint Myself in Woad* (David Antony Clark), on *Dance!* UCA ltd. 2002. **Task 4** *Varied Waltz*, on *Springsound*. **Tasks 3, 7** *Frog Ponds*, on *Springsound*. **Task 8** *Baroque 'n Droid*, (David Antony Clark), on *Dance!*

For relaxation and release: *Dead Can Dance the Serpent's Egg*, CAD C 808. *Ocean Dreams*, Dean Evenson, SP7140.

Web sites

www.danceuk.org – includes notes on the healthier dancer

www.alexandertechnique.com

www.feldenkrais.com

www.kdmmanagement.co.uk – Adventures in Motion Pictures, Matthew Bourne

www.dv8.co.uk – DV8 company

www.webindia123.com/dances/bharatanatyam

Chapter 3

HOW, WHERE, WHEN?

FROM TECHNIQUE TO DANCE

Technical training increases skill and precision. By now you may have learnt a set study and discussed why certain actions may have been chosen. It is obvious that there are other aspects of the movement, not just actions, which had to be selected. Not only the *what* but the *how*, the *where* and the *when*. When composing dance it is vital to select appropriate **dynamics**, **space** and **time**.

THE HOW – ENERGY (DYNAMICS)

The texture and the colour of dance gives it subtle meanings. Rudolf Laban analysed movement and much work in dance education draws on his ideas. He named certain aspects of weight, time, space and flow which can enrich your work:

- **TIME** . . . sudden – sustained

- **WEIGHT** . . . firm – light

- **FLOW** . . . bound – free

- **SPACE** . . . direct – flexible

Certain combinations of these give dance a specific look. For example, the tradition of classical ballet emphasises a sustained carriage of the body and an effortless lightness. This contrasts with the use of the opposites of contraction and release of the spine in the style of Martha Graham which emphasises a 'firmer', more bound, range of energy and a giving into the pull of gravity.

It is easy to think that the word energy simply means something like:

3.1 Margot Fonteyn as Aurora in THE SLEEPING PRINCESS *(1939)*

'for two and a half hours, loud, complex drum beats pound out
the story . . . the dancers smile constantly and display the kind of
energy that would have an average aerobics class begging for
mercy after ten minutes.'

Maggie Semple[1]

But this is too simple a view of the wide ranging use of dynamics in
dance. *How* a dancer moves expresses the wide spectrum of human
emotions, from jumping for joy to collapsing into depression.

---

[1] A review of *Siye Goli. African dance and Adzido*, in *Dance Theatre Journal* 10,1,
Autumn, 1992, p. 21.

Task 1

Choose one task from the list below and create a short solo in silence. Use all six Dance Actions – travelling, jumping, turning, gesture, stillness and falling – in your dance.

1. **TIME**: gradually changing from sudden to sustained movement compose a solo called 'The river – from source to sea.'
2. **WEIGHT**: quickly changing from firm to light movement, make a solo called, 'The rebellion goes up in smoke.'
3. **FLOW**: constantly changing from bound to free and back again, produce a solo called, 'The obstacle race.'
4. **SPACE**: using a broom and a piece of silk, create a solo which uses direct and flexible movement. Make sure the changes from one to the next are a part of the dance.

The terms *energy*, *force*, *dynamics* and *qualities* need to be clarified.

- **energy** is pure potential ever present ready to be used;

- **force** is the intensity of weight being used, ranging from firm to light;

- **dynamics** is force and time combined and results in combinations of sudden, sustained with light and firm.

- **efforts**, as named by Rudolf Laban. Thrust, flick, press, float, dab, glide, slash and wring arise from how the energy is applied, either directly or indirectly.

You can use a wide range of dynamics to produce many different *qualities* and expressions, for example:

- **swinging** – a heavy drop followed by a light suspension, appears free and natural.

- **vibrate** – sudden repeated percussive movements appear as a quiver, shake or tremble.

- **percussive** – sharp, sudden, direct impulses, eg strike, thrust, punch.

- **suspended** – breathless, weightless, soaring, eg at the top of a leap or balance.

- **collapse** – a total giving in to gravity, eg slow sink or fast fall which does not rebound.

Task 2

Divide the floor into a grid of four or six areas (chalk marks will do). As a group, allocate a landscape to each area, eg a strong gusty wind, a dark cave where spiders' webs brush your face as you walk, a floor covered with drawing pins, deep sticky mud, a thick jungle which you have to hack your way through, an earthquake etc. Make up some of your own. Travel around the room finding your own route and making clear changes in the dynamics and qualities with which you move from one area to another. When everyone has established their routes, try mixing and matching various couples or trios to see how they look together. Sometimes you may chance to find some which look interesting together – either because of their similarities or their contrasts.

Movement qualities invoke feelings and when a number are used together they convey more general meanings and sensations.

In Robert Cohan's *Waterless Method of Swimming Instruction* he uses a great deal of sustainment and suspension to give the impression of floating in water.

Christopher Bruce chooses powerful, strong intense qualities for the ghosts in *Ghost Dances*. These menaces loom over the livelier, light folk steps of the mortal world which in turn are transformed into ghostly, slow sustained walking steps after their violent deaths. The three contrasting qualities confront us, the audience, with the needless taking of life in the violent regimes of South America.

Lea Anderson in the videodance for The Cholmondeleys and the Featherstonehaughs, *Cross Channel*, uses contrasts in dynamics. The sunbathers' gestures are lazy, heavy and bound in the oppressive heat, in contrast to the bouncy, free and lively trampolinist in the background. Together they paint a witty picture of a day at the beach.

There is a wide range of dynamics in *Memory and Other Props*, (Shobana Jeyasingh 1998), starting gradually and gently, then shifting up to top gear with a much more sudden and stronger range. These shifts occur throughout the dance and seem to set a picture of a mind in quiet reflection on the past, contrasted with memories flashing by.

3.2 WATERLESS METHOD OF SWIMMING INSTRUCTION (1974), choreography Robert Cohan for the London Contemporary Dance Theatre

THE WHERE – SPACE

'I looked to space as a potential three-dimensional canvas'
Alwin Nikolais[2]

Designing dance in space is essential. The way in which movement and dancers are positioned must be appropriately chosen to make the expression of the dance clear. Space is alive in dance. It is like an invisible partner: it can surround you, pulsate, be an opponent to be pushed away.

In ballet, design in space can be pure visual delight for its own sake. Mary Wigman, an early German modern dancer, would use space as an active element. If we are to understand how she did this, and indeed to make use of space in this way, we must break down space into its components.

---

[2] *Vision of Modern Dance*, ed. Jean Morrison Brown, p. 116.

3.3 EMBRACE TIGER AND RETURN TO MOUNTAIN *(1968), choreography Glen Tetley, for Rambert Dance Company*

Personal Space and General Space

Siobahn Davies's *New Galileo* (LCDT 1984) began with small movements which gradually enlarged to fill the stage. This is a clear example of using the extremes of personal and general space to make a statement. In everyday life we carry our own personal 'space bubble' with us and feel uncomfortable if someone invades this by coming too close, but in dancing we break the usual space distance rules for visual or dramatic impact.

In Glen Tetley's *Embrace Tiger and Return to Mountain* (Rambert 1968), the opening section fills the stage with dancers placed space bubble distance apart as they go through their ritual *T'ai chi* meditations. Even though they are separate in space and time their identical movement phrases create a strong feeling of unity and strength. Later, duets bring the dancers very close to each other with a great deal of touch and shadowing. We sense their agitation as their bubbles are invaded.

Task 3

SHADOWS. In twos, one leads the other and becomes a second skin – as close as possible. Travel, change level. As the sun sinks the shadow lengthens and moves further away. You still feel connected even though the space is between you. Change roles through a smooth natural transition.

3.4 Tightrope Dance Company (1980), choreography Linda Ashley

Level

In early modern dance techniques like that of Martha Graham, a low earthy feel was emphasised as a reaction against the verticality and constant lift of classical ballet. The middle or medium level is our everyday 'feet on the ground' state. It is from here that we explore the possibilities of using all three levels, high, medium and low, in their extremes; falling, jumping and lifting each other.

Robert Cohan's use of the ladder in *Hunter of Angels* (1967) illustrates well the use of levels to reinforce the images of heaven, earth and hell in the struggle between twins Jacob and Esau and the angel.

Task 4

The whole group start outside the space with a variety of musical percussion instruments. These are played in response to the movement and dancers may respond to the sounds.

1. In your own time, dancers run into the space and fall, quickly rise without stopping and continue or exit.
2. As for (1) but very slowly with stillness on low levels.
3. Combine (1) and (2) and relate to the other dancers by echoing, shadowing, matching and mirroring them.
4. Travel into the space on a high level to take a still shape on a high, low or medium level and exit immediately. Emphasise shapes which respond to dancers already in the space, ie either copy, complement or contrast. Try to travel in many different ways.
5. Repeat (4) but include chairs, boxes, platforms etc and contact between dancers, eg assist a jump, help up from a fall and so on.

Direction, Dimension and Plane

Some images are expressed through **direction**, eg a backward retreat, a forward chase or race, uncertain sideways sidling. See the contrast between groups of dancers making up forward, marching armies and those forming a backwards scuttling cluster.

Dimensions are the result of joining two directions:

- **Depth** – forward and backward; advance and retreat

- **Width** – side to side; open and close

- **Height** – up and down; rise and sink

Lea Anderson's use of height dimension and tiny gestures within Personal space is distinctive to her style.

Planes are the result of joining two dimensions:

3.5 SODA LAKE (1981), choreography Richard Alston, dancer Mark Baldwin

- **Vertical** – height and width
- **Horizontal** – width and depth
- **Sagittal** – depth and height.

Task 5

Egyptian Frieze. Within large groups – one person takes a shape emphasising the vertical plane in two dimensions, height and width. People join in one at a time in response to the design as it grows, ie varying level, closeness etc.

Compose a solo dance called 'The Amazing Moving One-legged Table' emphasising the horizontal plane.

Interesting examples of the use of direction, dimension and planes can be found in *Soda Lake* by Richard Alston and Martha Graham's *Frontier* (1935).

Soda Lake was a solo performed in silence. It takes the theme of a vast American landscape as seen through the eyes of sculptor Nigel Hall. The dance relates to the sculpture in dimension, direction and shape. Travelling on the floor clearly uses depth in advancing towards and retreating from the sculpture, like the lines of a landscape painting, or of the sculpture itself. At one point the movement echoes the depth and height of the sculpture.

Alston started his training with London Contemporary Dance School and so would have worked in the Graham style. Interestingly, Martha Graham's solo *Frontier* uses a simple set designed by Isamu Noguchi which consists of two ropes and a fence, putting the dancer in the vast American wild west. It has to do with plains and distances. It's about roads that disappear into the distance or a railroad track. It uses simple movements like rising and sinking, forward advances, travelling with large circular gestures in the air, opening and closing and small flexible twists. The isolation of the lone woman on her ranch miles from anywhere is expressed clearly and strongly.

Shape, Space Patterns

The shape of movement in space can make patterns:

1. in the air;
2. on the floor
3. as the overall body shape.

These may be curved, circular, flowing, graceful, lyrical and can be felt as soft, caring, reflective, soothing and natural. Straight, sharply angular patterns tend to imply mechanistic, imposing, aggressive themes.

In *Soda Lake* the circular gestures are used to make an air pattern which Alston calls 'tracing the shapes'. It is performed under the hoop and echoes the circle shape. Another gesture is a curved arm which follows and traces the straight line of the vertical pole.

Task 6

Choose one of each type of pattern and travel along it on the floor, first with similar body shapes and air patterns, then with contrasting ones. How does this feel and what are the possible ways it changes the expression?

Standard   Free Form

Body Shape

Symmetrical or asymmetrical: *Symmetry*, ie the same both sides, produces feelings of stability, control and authority. *Asymmetry* produces tension, unpredictability and contrast. In dance one can be used to emphasise the other. Too much of either one can be monotonous.

A huge variety of body shapes are possible. They may be roughly categorised as four types; wide and flat like a *wall*; curled up like a *ball*; long and straight like a *ruler*; contorted and *twisty*. You could experiment with holding these four shapes whilst doing the six Dance Actions. Be prepared for some amusing challenges.

Task 7

The Robot. In pairs, imagine one of you is a prototype robot and the other is operating you by remote control, but you can only move one side of the body at a time, asymmetrically. The operator calls out body parts and instructions such as *sit, lie down on your front, side or back, stand, travel,* etc.

Discuss how this felt. What does it tell you about human movement? What felt difficult and why?

In Cohan's *Hunter of Angels*, symmetry of the duo's body shapes in mirroring is used to show the relationship of the twin brothers.

3.6 *L'APRÈS MIDI D'UN FAUNE (1913), Vaslav Nijinsky*

In 1913 Vaslav Nijinsky set new standards in classical ballet technique with his high leaps, but he also shocked audiences with a revolutionary choreography, as in the ballet *L'Après Midi d'un Faune*. To music by Debussy and design by Leon Bakst the influence of Greek friezes on the movement broke all the traditional rules of ballet. Limbs were held parallel to give a flat asymmetric look, as in figures portrayed on Greek vases.

The Stage Space

Do dancers control the space or does the space control the dance? Traditional ballet choreographers – and some modern dance ones too – use the stage space according to set criteria of staging such as the strength of the centre spot and of the diagonal from upstage right to downstage left. Not all choreographers use this method. Merce Cunningham ignored it in favour of treating all areas as equal and leaving the audience to decide what to look at first. In his dance *Tread* (1970), lines of electric fans on poles divide the space at the front of the stage. The audience chooses either to watch the spaces between the poles, or how one dancer passes between and around them, or the entire stage.
Some general rules about the stage space:

1. Stage right and left are from the performer's position. For the audience it is the other way round.
2. Traditionally, centre stage is the most powerful place and the upstage right to downstage left diagonal is the strongest.
3. Action at the front tends to be more humorous.
4. Action at the back tends to be more distant in space and time.

The term *facing* means the placing of the body in relation to the front of the stage (*downstage*), so that the audience sees it at the best angle. For example consider this shape placed at different angles.

a)   b)

Which would you choose as least and which as most clear?   67

These kinds of considerations can be explored on computer these days. There are software programmes such as *Life Forms*, developed by Thecla Schiphorst, which animate the human body. Merce Cunningham choreographed *Biped* in 2002 using this method. He describes his computer explorations:

'... one can make up movements, put them in the memory ... This can eventually be examined from any angle.'

Merce Cunningham[3]

As already stated this conventional theatrical style was experimented with in the 1960s and 70s. Nowadays dance is using more untraditional spaces. This brings with it different concerns when spacing and placing the dancers for the audience. Siobhan Davies's *Plants and Ghosts* (2002) toured in non-theatrical venues such as a deserted air base, a warehouse and an art gallery. The audience was seated deliberately much closer to the dance than would be the case in a theatre. This brings the viewer up close with some of the small details of the movement and the shifts in the dancers' steps and muscles, which are characteristic of her style. Therefore by her unconventional use of the 'stage' space she has drawn the audience's attention to see her choreographic style more effectively. More recently video and TV have influenced dance and pieces are composed especially for this medium, the modern technology producing rich and spectacular interplay of movement and space. Lloyd Newson's daring *My Sex Our Dance* has been adapted for video. There is more about dance for screen in Chapter 8.

Task 8

1. Create a dance in the round called 'Circle Ritual'.
2. Discuss the various spaces which you are familiar with and that the whole or part of the group may improvise in, eg a playground, a beach, a weights room, a corridor, a garden, a football pitch etc. Be aware of all the different sights and sounds that may affect your movement. Decide where the audience might be to provide them with clear sight lines.

[3] www.merce.org/technologylifeforms

3.7 TREAD (1970), *choreography Merce Cunningham*

3.8 MY SEX OUR DANCE (1987), *choreography Lloyd Newson for DV8*

You can choose how to use space to convey your ideas most advantageously. The possibilities are endless – make sure you do not lose your way!

THE WHEN – TIME AND RHYTHM

Time is passing us every day. We sense it through a *pulse*, ie a repeated beat that marks rhythm and gives order. As a dancer you must be able to keep time accurately. The sense of rhythm often determines dance styles such as Jazz, Indian, African or Flamenco.

Pulse and Tempo

The pulse of a heart beat is a sign of life and measures time. It underlies all our movements. Pulse can vary in speed. Five minutes of a movement at a slow tempo can seem longer than five minutes of a movement at a fast tempo.

Task 9

One person times one minute on a stopwatch for the group. They move as slowly as possible for what they estimate is a minute. They must stop when they think a minute is up, however long it takes. Repeat with fast movement. How accurate was their estimate? How different did the two tempi feel?

A slow, leisurely waltz feels and looks smooth and lyrical unlike a fast one which is animated and lively. Speed or tempo affects the mood, feeling or quality of a dance.

Acceleration is an increase in tempo; *Deceleration* is a decrease in tempo. You can build interest by increasing tempo, strength and size, like crescendos in music. Similarly, quieter sections can be made to emphasise softer, smaller moments. The contrast of these two builds sections in the dance, giving overall pace and form.

In Robert North's *Death and the Maiden* the tempo increases and decreases of Schubert's music are reflected in the moments of dramatic intensity and the sections building up to them. The maiden dances frantically around the space to a particular section of fast music, hopelessly meeting death at every turn, unable to escape her fate.

Accent

An accent in rhythm is a stress on one or more beats. Try clapping the following, accenting the clap marked ∨:

$$\overset{\vee}{1}2345678/\overset{\vee}{1}2345678/\overset{\vee}{1}234/\overset{\vee}{1}234/\overset{\vee}{1}2/\overset{\vee}{1}2/\overset{\vee\vee\vee\wedge\vee}{1}23\;4$$

$3\overset{\wedge}{\;}4$ indicates to clap the off-beat. Now try the above in movement, say with opening and closing, rising and sinking or walking with changes of direction. Accents can shift to create surprise, or, if spaced further apart, give a solemn dignified mood. Conversely if accents occur close together a more vivacious, urgent mood is achieved.

Task 10

Try to create a phrase of six triplets where the accent is always shifting from one to two to three in an unexpected order. Be clear how you create the accent, eg clap or tilt the torso suddenly; make an arm gesture; change level etc.

Metrical Rhythm

In most western music, phrases of beats are divided into measures occurring at regular intervals. The number of beats in a measure is the metre and this gives regular timing to support, play off or contrast against the movement. The top part of a time signature shows how many beats form a measure and the bottom number indicates the kind of note that receives one count;

2/4: indicates two beats in a measure and one quarter note receives one count.

Some movements fit more naturally into certain metres, for example regular swings fit usually in a 6/8 metre. Some metres are uneven and produce moods of comedy or tension in their asymmetry:

5/4 $1 2 \overset{\vee}{3} \overset{\vee}{4} 5$ or $\overset{\vee}{1} 2 3 \overset{\vee}{4} \overset{\vee}{5}$

7/4 $\overset{\vee}{1} 2 \overset{\vee}{3} \overset{\vee}{4} 5 6 7$ or $\overset{\vee}{1} 2 3 \overset{\vee}{4} \overset{\vee\vee}{5} 6 7$

When using strictly metered music, beware of letting the music dictate the rhythm. You can avoid this by accenting movement which clashes with the musical accent. Use different accents for different dancers. When the accent shifts to a usually *un*accented beat (*syncopation*) it can create a very exciting effect, especially if different dancers are syncopated against each other and the music. Similarly, more random movement creates rhythmical and visual tension.

Many choreographers show clear use of music and rhythmical styles. Richard Alston in *Dealing with Shadows* (1990) uses the sonata form of the music by Mozart. Alston's indisputable musicality also reflects the natural rhythms and qualities of his dancers.

In Robert North's *Troy Game*, breath rhythms give the movement its shape as well as the complex meters of the Brazilian *batacuda* music.

African dance is a genre in which rhythm is all-important. Dance and drumming go together in African culture. Several rhythms are played simultaneously, creating a complex blend to which the dancers respond when called by the master drummer.

The rhythmical skills of a Bharatha Natyam dancer must be precise. In this style of Indian dance the dancer determines the many possible rhythmic cycles, leading the musicians. This is especially so in the abstract sequences which demand virtuosity during improvisation. There is a jazz-like relationship of syncopated rhythms in the improvisations between the stamping feet, ankle bells, percussion instruments and song. A verse may be sung and danced several times in a row and each time the rhythms are explored as new.

Task 11

In a trio play the complex rhythm below on three different drums at the same time.

	1	2	3	4	5	6	7	8	9	10	11	12
A	1			4	5		7			10		
B		2	3		5	6		8		10		
C	1		3		5		7		9	10	11	12

accent where the numbers show, play softly in the blanks

You can experiment with this, adding more instruments etc. Use rhythmic work movements such as digging, laying railway tracks, bringing water etc to dance this.

Task 12

Walk in pairs to a moderate pulse. One dancer keeps the pulse while the other person walks, skips or takes any simple steps in double time. The person walking allows the other to keep up by changing length of stride, or floor pattern or direction.

Repeat, this time trying to establish a more interesting phrase of steps which is repeatable and keeps up with the walking partner.

In Task 12 we see a regular beat as supporting the less regular one. Regular beats such as a comforting, cradle-like rock, or a relaxing, hypnotic waltz can help to keep timing organised. When the beat becomes irregular it can be more difficult to organise but it is fun and challenging. It gives dance movement an element of surprise or shock, comic effect or irritation. Music from the far east can often sound discordant to us because of its different sense of rhythmic organisation. Try listening to some Balinese *gamelan* music – it would be an interesting source of accompaniment for your own dance compositions.

Nonmetrical Rhythms

Rhythm is all around you: in the sea, in your body (your heartbeat, breathing, walking) in machinery, in animals. Often these do not have a regular pulse but may speed up or slow down quite unpredictably. Dance movement sometimes has its own nonmetrical rhythm which may only relate to music by broadly going across the beat and can be performed in silence or with the accompaniment of breathing, stamping, clapping. These natural rhythms are just as strong as the more metric ones and are a vast treasure for the choreographer.

Task 13

1. Try to move continually falling (breathing in) and rising (breathing out) and vice versa. Discuss how different these actions feel.
2. Repeat (1) with wavelike movements, opening and closing, swinging.
3. Put together a solo where the breath leads and shapes the movement.
4. In threes, improvise with action and reaction using different sorts of breaths, eg sigh, blow, gasp. Form a short duet with a 'question and answer' structure.

In Glen Tetley's *Pierrot Lunaire* (1962), he is influenced by the structure of the Schoenberg score of the same name. A characteristic of Schoenberg's score is that, unlike more conventional works, it does not have many long phrases or much repetition. There are extremes of sudden, fast tempos which disappear into slow sections and broken rhythms. The results are more like natural, spontaneous and nonmetric rhythms than metered ones.

Nonmetrical rhythms from everyday movements are juxtaposed with the catchy intricate rhythms of gestures in Lea Anderson's *Cross Channel*. Her use of repetitive, but surprising, rhythms and dynamic phrasing is eye-catching and involving for the audience.

> '... there's a painterly exactness with which Anderson composes bodies in space and a rhythmic wit in her phrasing which ensures that however good the Featherstonehaughs may be for a laugh, the choreography is unquestionably serious dance.'
>
> *Judith Mackrell*[4]

[4] *Male-biting suspense*, in *The Independent*, 22.2. 1991.

Further Reading

Cheyney and Strader (1975) *Modern Dance*, Allyn and Baker Inc.
Ellfeldt, Lois (1974) *A Primer for Choreographers*, Dance Books.

Videos and DVD

From MJW Productions Ltd, London. Tel: 020 7713 0400 *Cross Channel*, Lea Anderson.
From www.dancebooks.co.uk *My Sex Our Dance*, DV8.
From the National Resource Centre for Dance www.surrey.ac.uk/NRCD *Hunter of Angels*, Robert Cohan.
From The Video Place; www.theplace.org.uk *Memory and Other Props*, Shobana Jeyasingh. On *Spring Re-Loaded 5*.

Music

Task 1 – *The Mission*, Ennio Morricone, Virgin (1986).
Music for Dance 3, Chris Benstead, PO Box 727, London SE13 3DX.
Task 5 – Penguin Café Orchestra, *Broadcasting from Home*, Virgin EGEDC 38.
From www.danz.org.nz On *New Zealand Music for Creative Dance*, selected by Jenny Cossey, 2001.
Task 8.1 – *Te Po* (Hirini Melbourne and Richard Nunns).
Task 8.2 – *Imbal Imbalan* (Megan Collins).

Web sites

www.art.net/~dtz – Thecla Schiphorst
www.credo-interactive.com – Life Forms
www.rambert.org.uk
www.sddc.org.uk – Siobhan Davies Dance Company

Chapter 4

DANCE COMPOSITION

FORMING AND FORM

'The work as a whole must be of one stuff, as an emerald is all
emerald – crush it to powder and each tiny pinch of that powder
will still be an emerald.'
Ted Shawn[1]

All arts arrange their elements in an orderly way with meaning and
purpose, whether organising the notes of music or the plot of a novel.
This process gives *form* and it is as basic to life itself as it is to art. It is
seen in the growth of a tree, the rising and setting of the sun, the cycle
of the seasons. Art uses form to help an idea grow, to support it and to
give it structure. It is the life within the dance which has grown naturally
from the stimulus, through improvisation and the shaping of phrases. In
dance, it is up to us to decide an appropriate order for the phrases and
all the components. In this way, phrases build up into larger units,
forming sequences. These sequences need to be logically developed so
that they have a beginning, middle and end.

FORMING THE MOVEMENT

Devices for dance composition

As you make dances you choose the what (actions), how, where and
when which are appropriate to the images you wish to express.
Arranging the order and pattern of the movements can be confusing.
How to start? What happens at the end? In dance there are rules to help
you organise your movements. These are not tricks of the trade but ways
to make more out of less, yet remaining within an overall plan.

---

[1] *Vision of Modern Dance*, p. 30.

1.1. Motif: the shaped phrases of movement are known as *motifs* and they contain the style and images of the dance. They are repeated, developed and varied so give the overall shape and expression (think about the emerald).

The simplest way to use a motif is to repeat it exactly on and off during a dance. However, if there is too much of this simple repetition the dance becomes more like a simple routine than an interesting choreography. There are other ways that motifs can be woven through a dance. These are *variation* and *development*.

1.2. Motif variation: keeping the order of the movements in a motif the same you could vary the action, time, space and dynamics of the motifs. Here are some examples:

- Add another Dance Action; to travelling add some arm gestures;

- Vary the size of the movement; larger to smaller;

- Change the level; from medium to high;

- Alter the focus; from going with the direction to against it;

- Change the direction; from forwards to backwards;

- Adjust the quality; what was a swing becomes a sustained movement;

- Vary the tempo; from fast to slow.

Task 1

In a group of four compose a motif together which uses three of the six Dance Actions. Each one of you varies it by changing the mood and dynamics e.g. lyrically, sneakily, lively, angrily. Perform the original motif together, then show each variation in turn.

A fine example of this is Doris Humphrey's *Water Study* (1928), in which the dancers' backs are wavelike and varied by firstly a gradual increase of force which sweeps them across the stage. Then the force decreases leading to the final stillness.

Task 2

Watch *Boy*, choreographed by Rosemary Lee on the *Best of Spring-dance Cinema 96*. Even though this is a dance made for film it still uses the devices of motifs. Near the start the boy (Tom Evans) runs from left to right across the screen. This travelling motif appears several times later on. See if you can spot it and describe how it is varied.

1.3 Motif development: involves making more extreme and complex changes to a motif. Unlike variation the order of the movements may change. Although the motif will still be recognisable it may result in quite a change of appearance. Here are some examples, motifs may:

- Reverse the order of the movements;
- Be fragmented so that parts of one motif are mixed with those of another;
- Embellish a motif, decorating it with much more detail;
- Combine the above *and* variations.

You will need to experiment with these kinds of changes to motifs lots of times before finding ones which work the best.

Task 3

Working individually use the motif and variations from Task 1. Make a second motif which uses the other three of the six Dance Actions. Find ways of developing the motifs from the bullet list above to make a short solo entitled *Mood Swings*.

2. Transition: within the individual motifs and in between the motifs, sequences and sections of the dance there must be links known as *transitions*. These transitions can vary in complexity. They can be gradual or sudden, they can overlap. Above all they must not be allowed to hide the material of the main movement.

Robert Cohan's *Waterless Method of Swimming Instruction* uses the simple idea of entries and exits from the pool to link the sections of the dance fluently. The use of transition is not always so clear; there are those who choose to break the rules, as did Merce Cunningham in 1953. In his dance *Septet*, the dancers' entrances and exits at the end of each section use ordinary movements such as shaking hands and nods of goodbye. This odd technique draws attention to the gaps in between the sections, making the transitions as significant as the main dance.

Task 4

Compose two motifs which contain very different actions and qualities, eg

- fast jumps and swings
- sustained turns and gestures.

Experiment with them in the five ways listed below:

1. with a fast, abrupt link;
2. overlap them, ie start the second motif during the end of the first;
3. make a complicated phrase to link them;
4. use a segment of each of them to make the link;
5. find a smooth efficient way to link them.

Show each other your ideas and discuss which ones worked the best and why. Be ready for some surprises!

---

3. Highlights: certain moments of the dance will stand out as being most memorable. This can be achieved by playing with the action, dynamics, space or time; by adding, changing or contrasting and making movement stronger/lighter, longer/shorter, and so on. By placing highlights carefully you can express the intention of your dance more clearly to the audience.

In Paul Taylor's *Aureole* (1962) the delicate movement is highlighted by the unexpected, for example one dancer exits doing bouncy jumps then re-enters followed by another and returns again in a bouncy trio. This is a lovely example of building to a highlight. The final section of the dance is a more complicated version of itself. It exaggerates and decorates the original movement by distorting shapes which were previously straight or angular into zig-zags, turned-in or flexed. The tempo also crescendos to a headlong, seemingly frantic and out-of-control pace. Even the space is disturbed by emphasising the upstage left, downstage right diagonal which was not used in the earlier section. Taylor rushes the whole form into a crushing finale with great impact.

4. Climax: as noted above *Aureole* built up to a strong finale as an ending. The *climax* was the end, but sometimes it happens just before the actual finish of the dance. In the Ballet *The Nutcracker* (1892) the climax is the Waltz of the Flowers, but not the end. The last section is a traditional *apotheosis,* where dancers take turns in a kind of prolonged curtain call. The soloists are last and honoured, a little like the ruling monarch of the court in the 1600s who would appear as the god Apollo or the sun after the dance itself was ended.

Similarly in the videodance *Cross Channel* the dance builds to its crescendo when the men and women finally meet up for the party in the beach hut. The dancing and partying are really hotting up as, unknown to the dancers, the tide comes in. The sea tips the hut up onto its side. Bang – climax! There is a transitionary moment's pause, assisted by a change of shot by the camera to the outside of the hut, then the dance continues. Lea Anderson crawls out of the door (now on the top of the hut), looks around to assess the damage, closes the door and as the champagne cork pops the party continues. They're now dancing up the walls and the music fades into the early hours.

Task 5

In a solo use the following movements:

- running
- falling
- jumping
- stillness
- gentle arm gestures.

Create highlights:

- repeat one movement more times each time you do it;
- gradually decrease or increase the size of one of the movements each time you do it;

- suddenly interrupt one of the movements, for example the run with a stillness.

Show your solo to a partner and allow them to comment on whether or not these highlights hold their interest. Consider questions like:

Was there enough build up?
Were some highlights more important so that they became climaxes?

---

5. Contrast: *contrast* provides variety but it is a special type, introducing as it does new material. This could be a new point of view, a totally different quality or an obvious break from the central concern. The new movement may happen within established motifs, or it may be an entirely new motif. In the first half of the videodance *Boy* the motifs use travelling, arm and hand gestures, jumping, falling and rolling. The contrasting motifs which then appear take on animal images: birds pick their way through the marram grass; horses gallop along the sand and they even chew the grass!

In *The Dream* (1964), Frederick Ashton showed his fine choreographic skills in the constant fluid shifts between contrasting movement material. These were highly effective to show changes in mood and character. They included romantic love duets, slapstick comedy, flickering flying fairies and the earth bound clumsy (even when on pointe) character Bottom.

6. Chance: the pioneers of chance process as a device can be found in the music of John Cage and his partner, choreographer Merce Cunningham. Chance uses coincidence or fate to produce content and form perhaps by the throw of a dice, coins, anything. The dice may even be thrown during performance to decide which phrases of movement will be danced in which order – in this way the dance will be different each time it is performed. Task 8 in Chapter 2, based on actions, used this device.

The device of *chance* can also become the actual structure of a dance. It is a useful tool to have. You may have found some motifs but are unsure how to organise them in time and space. Sometimes just trying a few ideas at random may help you find the best solution to your physical puzzle.

Task 6

Find a short fairy story and cut it up into words, phrases or sentences. In a group of three or four, distribute the lines randomly and read the rearranged version. Each person takes a section of this and creates a brief dance from the words in any way they choose to abstract. (You may decide to read the words as accompaniment). Watch each other, then dance them in random order. You can create a group dance by learning each other's phrases and weaving in and out in any way you feel may work. Try to ensure that the group dance holds together in its transitions, highlights, variety, contrast.

Structures for dance composition

These are set models that have been found to work well in the arts; classical frameworks which can be found in music, art and literature. They determine the overall structure of a dance but the movement material within this may be shaped by any of the previous devices. These structures are known as *sequential, contrapuntal, narrative* and *natural*, and they can be mixed.

Sequential structures

These have sections which follow each other in a definite order. Each section has a theme and is identified by a letter. A is the first, B the second and so on. The sections have unity by sharing something common to both sections.

1. AB Form

The simplest form, consisting of theme (A) and a contrasting or developed theme (B) linked by a transition called a *bridge*. Obviously this provides repetition, variety, contrast and transition.

2. ABA Form

Again, this form gives order, consisting of a theme (A), developed or contrasting section (B) and return to the first theme (A). This gives a simple, well balanced structure.

Cyclical or loop form, (ending where you started) is common in African dance. It is used in *So What!*, (Badejo Arts, 2000) when the dance returns to some of the first motifs and finishes in the opening stillness.

3. ABACADA – Rondo Form

The A theme is first stated, then keeps returning in pure or varied form after related or contrasting themes are shown. A must be interesting enough to stand repetition. It is an easily enjoyable form because of its balance of repetition, variation and contrast. It is a typical form for many folk songs and dances, and is used in *Sergeant Early's Dream* by Christopher Bruce.

Bruce also uses this structure in his *Ghost Dances*. The ghost motifs open the whole dance and return after each section. Expressively they are used to emphasise the ever present fear, death and despair which the people of Chilé had to struggle against during the military dictatorship of the 1970s.

4. Theme and variation: This is similar to motif variation but is more complex because each variation may build on the previous one. Consequently the motif becomes increasingly 'genetically modified', until finally it may be just a very faint echo of the original.

Task 7

Find a short piece of folk music, for example from Ireland or South America and listen to it. Divide it into sections – A, B, C etc. Compose a dance reflecting the simple structure of the music. Take care with the transitions between the sections and appropriate use of repetition, variation and contrast. It may help to use movements like simple steps, changes of direction and jumps.

Contrapuntal structures

Like the sequential ones, contrapuntal structures are found in music. These have a single theme which plays against itself, against one or more other themes or is woven through the entire length of the piece. Two or more strands are being heard or seen at the same time and so it can create a complex structure. The theme motif needs to be very clear and obvious to an audience so that the motif and how it is varied can be detected and appreciated throughout the piece. There are three principal contrapuntal structures:

1. Bass ground – A single theme is the opening statement which repeats through the whole piece while other themes play against its rhythmical pattern. In dance it is useful for themes which involve group opposition, inevitability, tenacity or a solo figure versus a group. It is challenging to dancers because of the rhythmic variety possible.

2. Round or canon – A round consists of a simple melody which is imitated and repeated against itself at different intervals. The melody is the same in all parts, whereas in a canon the original theme is often developed or varied.

3. Fugue – This makes interesting dance even though it is complicated and irregular. The main theme interweaves with counter themes and, as in motif development, the melody (movement) can be inverted, reversed, shortened, slowed down, lengthened. The fugue usually builds to an exciting climax then quietens to a softer repetition of the opening. It can be valuable in developing dramatic ideas. Ian Spink used a fugue composed by Bach to transform a play into an abstract dance. Ordinary gestures such as picking up the telephone are repeated in strict rhythm and so become strange and surreal. The movements are developed like a fugue, each part eventually coming together to create something new.

Task 8

In groups of four, find motifs which use cooking actions (eg whisk, stir, chop). Make one motif four counts and describe only one cooking action, another for six counts using two cooking actions; the third for 12 counts and using as many cooking actions as possible. Adding other movement where appropriate to create exits and entrances, compose a dance called 'Mad Chefs'. Give the dance three sections; one is Bass ground; another a Round and the last a Fugue.

Other dance composition structures

1. Narrative structure

Both modern dance and ballet use stories for content and structure. The plot can be made more exciting by the characters, locations, flashbacks, dreams and dance easily conveys fantasy, memory and nightmares. Short stories, autobiographies, your own diary, myths, fables all provide rich stimulus and a ready way of forming a dance. They can also exploit psychological effects as in Graham's *Errand into the Maze* (1947) where we see the heroine's journey into a maze and confrontation with the minotaur as told in the Greek legend. At the same time it signifies an exploration of her own fears and doubts.

This structure uses sections or episodes, as in a soap opera, to follow characters along a time line.

Another example is Matthew Bourne's *Cinderella* (1997). This follows on the nineteenth century classical ballet story-telling tradition, but is in a post-modern style. The original romantic story is retold to make the audience think about life in the twenty-first century. Stereotypes such as the icon of goodness, the Fairy Godmother, are danced by a male dancer. Similarly the Ugly Sisters, traditionally danced by men and symbols of evil, are performed by women. The narrative is the same act by act, but the social stereotypes are quite different to the original. Other choreographers who work in a similar style are Mats Ek and Mark Morris.

The ease of change of location that filming and editing brings allows the videodance *Cross Channel* to tell a story of a weekend holiday in a short amount of time.

2. Collage

This structure is rather like the one used in visual art, when a collection of images are 'thrown' together. They are loosely related, but not necessarily connected in a time line, so it does not tell a story in the usual sense. It is more like a dream world and can be quite surreal (beyond the real), even nightmarish. Work by Pina Bausch and Lloyd Newson often use this structure. Bausch is regarded by many as one of the twentieth century's leading choreographers, because she expanded the possibilities for theatre dance. Her work is described as:

'. . . Meticulously unstructured and freeform, the works themselves lack any of the usual, reassuring reference points such as plot, character, even coherent meaning . . .'

John O'Mahony[2]

3. Natural structures

The natural world can give structure and form to dance. Images such as day and night, seasons and life cycles (a butterfly or human) can easily stimulate improvisation and provide a structure.

An example of this is Paul Taylor's *Orbs* (1966). The six parts include Venusian Spring, Martian Summer, Terrestial Autumn and Plutonian Winter and the dancers are cast as planets and moons. Taylor symbolised the sun. He explored the cycle of the seasons and wove in the feeling of the strength of natural forces over which humans have no control.

The structure of *Four Scenes* (1998) by Christopher Bruce uses the natural process of four stages of human life from birth to death, and the piece takes places within the passing of one day from sunrise to sunset.

OVERALL FORM – UNITY

Drawing together the ideas of this chapter it becomes clear that as you compose you must be aware of certain ingredients:

- clear movement phrasing;
- logical development of chosen image(s) and motifs;
- balance of repetition, variation and development;
- providing sufficient contrast.

With sufficient attention to these concerns the dance will begin to show a clear overall structure and form. This may determine whether the dance has a slow lyrical nature or moves along quickly and athletically. Some dances fall into contrasting sections so it is important to 'pace' the composition. A gradual preparation for the main highlight of the dance, the *climax*, is a part of the pacing process. An appropriate balance of the proportions of the dance's sections, highlights and transitions will lead

---

[2] *Dancing in the dark*, in *The Guardian*, 26 January 2002.

towards an inevitable ending for the dance. This may be a return to the opening, an end to the story, highly energised, a fade out or into stillness, but whatever you choose it must be decisive and evolve from the rest of the dance. Remember it will be the last thing that the audience will see so it must be worth watching. The overall form of the finished dance will meet the needs of the choreographer's ideas, the performers and the audience.

Making dances is often considered to be like problem-solving. Searching for, finding and balancing all the parts of the solution to these physical puzzles will take time, but should result in a dance which is an expressive whole. If during the composition process, devices, structures and overall form are chosen appropriately for the images and ideas that are being expressed, a dance will have *unity*. The processes of composing and of rehearsing dances, to bring them to a standard when they are ready for performance, are further examined in Chapter 8.

THE COMPOSITION PROCESS

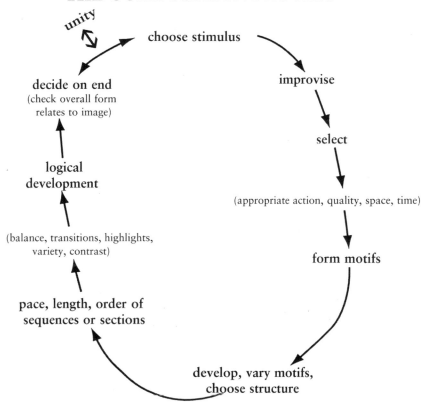

unity

choose stimulus

improvise

decide on end
(check overall form
relates to image)

select

logical
development

(appropriate action, quality, space, time)

(balance, transitions, highlights,
variety, contrast)

form motifs

pace, length, order of
sequences or sections

develop, vary motifs,
choose structure

REFERENCES

Further Reading

Cohen, Selma Jane (1966) *The Modern Dance, Seven Statements of Belief*, Wesleyan University Press.
H'Doubler, Margaret N. (1974) *Dance: A Creative Art Experience*, University of Wisconsin Press.
Humphrey, Doris *The Art of Making Dances*, Grove Press.

Music

Tasks 1 and 3 – *Yin Yang*, Radha Sahar on *Dance!*
Task 4 – *Shadows Falling*, on *Springsound*, Michelle Scullion.
Task 5 – Philip Glass, *Dance Pieces* CBS NK 39539.
Task 6 – *Space to Dream*, Radha Sahar on *Dance!*
Task 7 – *Mare's Wedding*, on *Dance!*
Task 8 – *Cook Island Rhythms*, Faipoto Aporo on *Dance!*

Videos and DVD

Available from www.dancebooks.co.uk: *Boy*, on *The best of Springdance Cinema 96*. Co-prod: *Arts Council of England* and *the BBC TV*. Directed Peter Anderson.
Dead Dreams of Monochrome Men, DV8 Physical Theatre, Lloyd Newson.
Sleeping Beauty, Mats Ek for the Cullberg Ballet, 2000.
From The Video Place: www.theplace.org.uk *So What!*, Badejo Arts. On *Spring Re-Loaded 6*.

Web sites

www.cullbergballet.com
www.pina-bausch.de

Chapter 5

GROUP DANCE

MORE THAN A SOLO

So far we have considered dance composition mainly as the creation, shaping and forming of movement from a chosen stimulus. One of the most enjoyable aspects of dance is dancing with others in a duet or group. However, when composing for more than one dancer additional issues need to be considered.

> 'Speaking beyond the movement for each individual dancer is the movement throughout the whole piece, and throughout all the parts that make the structure.'
>
> *Twyla Tharp*[1]

PARTNER WORK

In a duet each dancer is essential to the whole. It is not a solo for two people but involves communication – simple visual design, contact, moving at the same time and in conversation with each other. The involvement between the two allows relationships to be organised in different ways:

- leading and following;
- questioning and answering;
- meeting and parting;
- symmetry and asymmetry;
- matching and mirroring;
- contrast and complement;
- physical contact;
- co-operation and confrontation.

---

[1] Twyla Tharp, *The Dance Makers*, Elinor Rogosin, Walker and Co. 1980, p. 139.

Robert Cohan's *Hunter of Angels* is a duet based on the relationship of the twins Jacob and Esau. It uses mirrored movement to emphasise their twin relationship. It also uses contact between the dancers to make an interesting struggle.

Frederick Ashton was famous for romantic duets such as those in *The Dream*. The *Nocturne* pas de deux, for the King and Queen of the Fairies, Oberon and Titania, is full of love and passion. Starting in confrontation and contrast eventually they become complementary in a series of meetings and partings. Gradually they settle their argument harmoniously. Her sudden sharp movements slowly melt as they rediscover their love for each other. Ashton contrasts her dynamics with the stronger Oberon. At one point Oberon soothes Titania by rocking her from side to side, and at another the energy of her strong, proud arabesque swoons at his touch.

Task 1

In pairs:

1. Face your partner. Mirror each other with easy repeated movements and stillnesses, then make faster, more complicated phrases. Try to keep going as quickly and yet as accurately as possible. This will probably result in your varying on your partner's movement and can produce some interesting results.

2. One dancer is the clay and the other the sculptor. Mould the clay into many shapes. Develop this into impulses so that it becomes pushing/pulling, the passive person following the other into swing, rise, fall, roll, etc. If you are the passive dancer try not to anticipate, let your partner do the moving for you.

Task 2

Look at the photograph of *The Strange Party* and notice the following groups left to right:

1. Three figures in masks, dress suit, glittery costume and cape.

90

2. Pierrot surrounded by three young girls.
3. Two masked females in fancy dress.

Consider this description: 'The whole scene had a mysterious air of festivity.' Create a piece which starts with the groupings in the photograph and develop entrances, exits, different formations and so on.

SMALL GROUPS

Relationships

As well as the relationships listed as possible for duets, trios, quartets, quintets, sextets etc, give rise to even more possibilities of arranging relationships between the dancers. For example, in a trio combinations can be two versus one; all three together; one versus one versus one. Possible relationships between a trio of dancers are used very effectively in Christopher Bruce's *Swansong* (1987). This explores the injustices of political oppression and torture which such organisations as Amnesty International fight against. Set in the Chilean junta of General Pinochet in the 1970s the guards give an effective portrayal of the hot and cold,

5.1 THE STRANGE PARTY *(1981), choreography Linda Ashley*

question and answer interrogation routine in a two versus one relationship. Some sections of the dance are solos for the prisoner, as he is left to contemplate his fate. At these moments the guards are off stage, but the audience feels their presence and knows that the only escape from the cell is the final symbolic flight, as the prisoner's spirit escapes taking the truth with him. The guards are left without any information and we feel that a life was taken needlessly.

Similarly you can explore the possibilities of groups of any size. Remember, however, that the number of dancers you choose must be appropriate to the theme.

All the devices and structures for dance composition from Chapter 3 are enriched when used for groups. You should consider the number and placement on the stage of the dancers when developing motifs or when using structures such as ABA. The more dancers using the same motif the more impact there will be. This could also provide a strong background for a solo dancer presenting a contrasting or complementary theme.

ORGANISING GROUP MOVEMENT IN SPACE

Formations

There are many different possible group formations or shapes to choose from. Here are some possible ideas:

- lines – one behind the other, side-by-side;

- circles – facing inward, outward and around;

- wedges, triangles, diamonds, squares;

- close clusters and spread out scattered arrangements.

Each of these carries different meanings and can help you to express images and ideas in your choreography. For example, a military feel may be expressed by using formal lines and wedges of dancers advancing and retreating. In contrast the softer edges of close clusters alternating with dispersed, loosely scattered groups may express images of the natural world such as flocks of birds or shoals of fish. In fact, in this way an aquarium of shimmering shoals of fish is staged by twelve dancers in Siobhan Davies's *Carnival* (1982).

Once group shapes have been chosen you must decide where to put them on the stage. This, as previously mentioned in Chapter 3, can be a conventional design or a less formal arrangement which leaves the audience to select what to watch and when. The latter approach can lead to the use of less familiar venues such as parks and even roof tops!

Task 3

In a large group create and learn four short movement motifs. Organise two dances, one which uses clear group formations and the centre and diagonals, the other which scatters the dancers loosely around the stage. Watch the final result and discuss the differences.

Different types of formations in space often go with certain styles. For instance one would expect to see more formal lines in classical ballet such as Fokine's *Les Sylphides* than in modern works like Richard Alston's *Wildlife*. In these two very different dances, the way that groups are organised in space also relates to the way that the set is designed. The set of *Les Sylphides* is realistic and static in contrast to the constantly changing mobiles in *Wildlife*. The stage is also divided in very different ways which would obviously affect the group formations.

There are some interesting uses of formation in *Piano Variations* (1971) by Dutch choreographer Hans van Manen. His dances often explore power struggles in human relationships. Sometimes these are gender specific, as in *Piano Variations*, when a large group of female dancers appears in conflict with a solo male. The dance opens using a spread wedge formation. The women all face front and perform together the same motif of gestures, graceful ports de bras, elegant bends, stretches and dramatic falls. It is a solid, 'one for all and all for one' unit, several bodies but only one mind. The wedge formation emphasises their unity which appears supportive of each other and confrontational to outsiders. The spread wedge then gathers into a close cluster further emphasising their bond. The solo male can only watch, as they strut the catwalk he is the photographer. They form a leading and following line still ignoring him (a solo versus the group relationship). Their contained defiance frustrates him more and more as the dance goes on. Eventually his frustration becomes aggressive and he shadow boxes. Finally the women return to the original wedge and cluster, in so doing they enclose

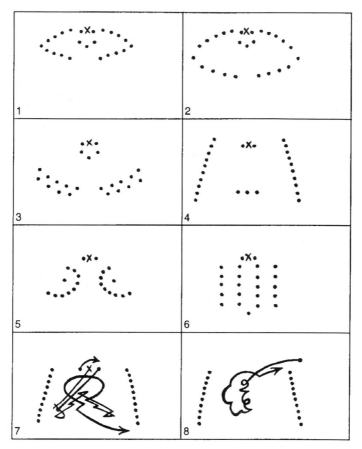

5.2 *LES SYLPHIDES (1909), choreography Mikhel Fokine. Fokine's group formations and floor patterns diagrams*

him. They seem to control him, as he is rocked into sleep by their controlling sway. Although there are no winners there is a sort of resolution, where overt aggression is not successful in taking power. Perhaps we are reminded that the hand that rocks the cradle rules the earth.

ORGANISING GROUP MOVEMENT IN TIME

One of the most satisfying ways of designing groups is to organise *when* dancers move. They may move all at the same time (in *unison*) or one after the other (in *canon*). Within these two structures there are many possibilities, leading to a rich variety of expression.

5.3 WILDLIFE *(1984), choreography Richard Alston, for Rambert Dance Company*

Unison

Dancers execute:

- the same movement at the same time;

- similar or complementary movement at the same time;

- contrasting movement at the same time.

Returning to *Piano Variations* we see how van Manen uses unison with formation to portray the tightly knit group. Unison is used in the opening and the second motifs, when dancers take on the look of catwalk models with strong clear walks and measured steps. In the third section of this ABA structure they repeat the original two motifs, then finally bring in the contrasting repetitive swaying in total unison to include the soloist as he conforms to their demands.

Lea Anderson frequently uses unison in side-by-side line formations. In her *Birthday* (1992), and its video version *Perfect Moment*, the dancers prepare for a big night out. They face front and make up their faces with small gestures in unison. It is a captivating image of a group fashion ritual. There is a similar unison in her *Flesh and Blood* when the dancers use tiny face and hand gestures to draw the air pattern spelling Joan. The overall result of this repetition, unison and formation is to add considerable fascination and to help the viewer to understand the themes of the dances. In both examples there is a feeling of importance of ritual, even though one is religious in purpose and other more connected to the importance of keeping up appearances. Or is Anderson asking if these are the same thing for some people?

Unison is often seen in classical ballet. The corps de ballet in *Giselle* (1841, Coralli and Perrot) dance as maidens who, abandoned by faithless lovers, have died before their wedding day, and are doomed to live as unhappy spirits or *wilis*, forever dancing by moonlight. Their unison gliding arabesque is an unforgettable haunting image.

When choreographers arrange dancers to do different movements at the same time the look is not quite so simple. In Matthew Bourne's *Swan Lake* the swans' large ensemble sections often feature small groups dancing complementary motifs in unison. The layering effect works successfully with the rich music to express the varying attributes of swans: strength, beauty, gentleness and violence. In an earlier part of this production the Royal Family go to the Opera House to watch the ballet. Bourne uses a contrasting unison here. The 'real' action is the hilarious comic parody of ballet, but meanwhile in the Royal Box the Prince's new common born girlfriend is enjoying herself in what the Queen considers to be unseemly behaviour. Eating sweets, applauding too much and giving the Queen a jolly good elbow in the ribs is all happening at the same time as the performance. The contrasting unison doubles the comic effect.

Canon

This type of movement may occur in strict order as each dancer in turn performs an entire motif like an echo. Each dancer stops moving when the motif is finished. This very simple canon can be made more interesting by overlapping movement so that each dancer starts before the one in front has finished. The dancers can also overlap motifs but finish at the same time, all doing the same thing.

5.4 *An overlapping canon*

5.5 THE MAD BAD LINE *(1990), choreography Linda Ashley. Canon rising onto one hand*

Another canon structure involves a group dancing the same motif at the same time but from different starting points. So one dancer may carry out counts one to eight whereas another may start at count six, ie 67812345 and so on. This can give a complex, dense and visually interesting look.

Van Manen's *Piano Variations* is an ABA structure and the canon of the 'B' section offers suitable contrast whilst still allowing 'B' to have something in common with 'A'. The new contrasting motif for the women is a sideways travel with a plié, which may look a little like a curtsey, but is quite assertive, not at all submissive to the man. It is danced in an *overlapping canon*, so for the first time they are not in unison but their solidarity still holds. It also contrasts because it is the first time that they allow him to be near to them. Then another and much greater contrast, which is a highlight of the dance, is that suddenly they remove their skirts, but they remain aloof from the man. Their attitude makes it clear that whatever they do is none of his business. This is what leads to his increasing frustration and the women's growing control. Consequently this use of canon and contrast gives a very satisfying and skilful ABA structure to the dance, as well as expressing the theme very clearly.

In Richard Alston's *Pulcinella* (1987) we see his characteristic style of complex canons and unison. It is also featured on the video *Essential Alston* (1998) and is clearly shown and explained in the *Brisk Singing* (1997) section.

5.6 ATOM SPLIT *(1981), choreography Linda Ashley*

Of course, all these canons can be developed and varied by using the same, similar or contrasting movement, and there is scope to add stillness, change level, direction, facing, stage placement, and to vary the quality and order of movements as well. Organising can be tricky. Persevere and experiment, because it will enrich your compositions.

Task 4

From the photograph entitled *Atom Split*, create a dance which depicts what happens just before and when **THE BOMB** is dropped. There are two main groups of dancers, the scientists and 'the rest'. Give these groups contrasting motifs. Compose a dance which concentrates on using various types of unison and canon. Movements which may be useful are:

- a vibration of hands and whole body
- slow uninterrupted walking
- running with sudden falls.

5.7 DANCESCAPES *(1983), choreography Linda Ashley, for Tightrope Dance Company*

Task 5

Watch a video of the first four minutes of Siobhan Davies's *White Man Sleeps* (1988) and note down as many examples of unison and canon as you can see. Compare notes with the rest of the group and try to explain how and why the timings succeeded.

GROUP TRUST AND CONTACT

The interest of group formations, placement and timings are emphasised by building trust between the dancers so that you can use contact. This is a special skill and a whole technique of dance has been created around it. It is called *Contact Improvisation* and was invented by American gymnast Steve Paxton, who later studied dance. Using his experience he produced a style based on giving and taking weight, on trusting someone to be there if you decide to fall or lean or bounce off them. In performance it is often improvised and emphasises natural movement, taking risk and responsibility for each other. Paxton was part of a dance revolution in the States in the 1960s which was based in Judson's Church, from which the group took their name.

Obviously this type of work requires practice like any other technique. Here are a few trust exercises that you may like to try and may give you confidence to use contact in your compositions.

Task 6

1. **The Circle of Trust**: One person stands in the centre of a close circle of five or six others. With feet glued to the centre spot, that person keeps the body straight and tilts off-balance towards the circle. The others gently take the weight and push the person back to the centre. Increase the size of the fall as confidence increases.

2. **Park Bench**: In twos, sit on a bench with arms touching, looking straight ahead. Alternate sitting and standing, trying to keep together as much as possible.

3. **Joint Journey**: In twos, travel the length of the room without loss of contact. Try to vary the way you travel and the parts of the body which

5.8 DEAD DREAMS OF MONOCHROME MEN (1988), *choreography Lloyd Newson for DV8*

are in contact. Include such actions as sliding, spinning, rolling, carrying, jumping, falling (and being caught!), lowering and lifting etc.

It is well worth experimenting in duets and larger groups with simple hand holds and counterbalances. Feel exactly how much or little energy is necessary for counterbalancing with someone else before the moment when balance is lost. Similarly other contact situations such as lifting, lowering, catching and throwing, supporting or assisted jumps can have exciting results. Improvise with rolling around on the floor softly, finding moments of stillness that give support to a partner in interesting shapes. The possibilities are many and when a higher level of competence is reached flying through the air to be caught by a partner, as in the dances of company DV8, may be possible.

Task 7

Below are a number of diagrams showing some duet support positions. Practise them singly trying to share the supportive positions. When confident arrange them in any order and link them with appropriate

movement and transitions. At first slowly then try to add faster, more explosive dynamics.

The first section of Siobhan Davies's *White Man Sleeps* uses contact work in the duets. The lifts and balances have soft, tender and easy dynamics. Similar contact technique may be seen in work by Belgian choreographers Anne Teresa de Keersmaeker, *Rosas danst Rosas* (1983) and Wim Vandekeybus, *What the Body does not Remember* (1987) but the dynamic is very different. They tend to use high risk, fast, furious and strong throws, catches and lifts in duets and small groups.

Shobana Jeyasingh uses an interesting and original mix of contact work with the ancient Indian classical dance style of Bharatha Natyam.

Sometimes you may be involved in a group making the dance with others and this can be satisfying and fun. When you dance in a piece there is a limit to what you see of its design and form, so you should also try to compose for other people without dancing in the composition.

Chapter 8 will give you more guidance on how to run successful rehearsals when making dance for performance.

REFERENCES

Video and DVD

Available from www.dancebooks.co.uk *Giselle*, the Kirov Ballet. *Grand Vizier*, Hans van Manen, a compilation of his dances. *Pulcinella* and *Essential Alston*, Richard Alston. *Rosas danst Rosas*, Anna Teresa de Keersmaeker. *White Man Sleeps* and *Wyoming*, Siobhan Davies.
Available from www.dancing-times.co.uk *Swansong*, Christopher Bruce.

Music

On *New Zealand Music for Creative Dance*.
Task 2 – *Other Echoes*, by Eve de Castro Robinson.
Task 4 – *Fax to Paris*, by Phil Dadson.
Task 7 – *Imbal Imbalan*, by Megan Collins.
On *Springsound*. Task 3 – *Driving Soft Rock*, Michelle Scullion.

Chapter 6

ACCOMPANIMENT FOR DANCE

When choosing what to use to accompany your dance it is tempting to choose your favourite band or singer, but often what you should ask is whether you need any sound at all. Ideally a composer would offer to write a score for you, note for note to match your dance, but if you are at school willing composers are probably a bit thin on the ground! That is why this chapter may help you to become aware of the many alternatives to that much heard statement, 'I cannot find any music.'

SOUND

Natural Sounds and Sounds from your Environment

These could be the sounds of a storm, a railway station, washing machine, birds, whale sounds, a football crowd. They can be mixed together with the sounds of musical instruments. This mixing creates *texture* as the characteristics of the different sounds combine. Robert Cohan's *Forest* (1977) is danced to an electronic score comprising wind in the trees, insects, birds, rain and thunder and was written after the choreography was completed. In an impressionistic style there is no story, but the atmosphere of the forest is created. The dance motifs reveal scenes of the echoing calls of the forest creatures as they appear fleetingly among the undergrowth and treetops.

Drosten Madden, who composes for Lea Anderson, uses a collage style of accompaniment. For *Bomb Around the Clock* (from *The Big Feature*, 1991) he superimposes the sound of roaring jet engines, like the ones of the B52 fighter aircraft which are mentioned in the lyric, over a bass line melody of the song *Rock Around the Clock*, by Bill Hayley.

Task 1

Take recordings outside in a busy street. Include sounds like footsteps, traffic, shops, trains etc. In a group of five or six devise a dance called

'Rush Hour'. Consider such ideas as a bus queue, fast walking patterns, supermarket shopping etc.

Vocal Sounds

A dance which uses live spoken accompaniment can emphasise and accent the images or the rhythms. The words may take a number of forms: melodic, song-like, disjointed, 'pure' sounds, breath, nonsense, in a different language.

Task 2

Choose one of Edward Lear's nonsense rhymes, a nursery rhyme or a poem by Lewis Carroll. Consider how you could develop its ideas to give movement phrases. Develop its rhythm, its images or its sounds for accompaniment. Make a trio from your movements.

In Richard Alston's *Rainbow Bandit* (1974) a sound collage of much repeated word phrases is gradually abbreviated and looped so that it becomes intensely rhythmic, and the motifs respond to this. Poetry and stories can be the dance stimulus as well as accompaniment, spoken by the dancers, a narrator or on tape.

In the first sections of the post modern *Time Lapses* (Sue Maclennan and Rosemary Lee, 2000) the performers' voices are the main part of the accompaniment. Gradually a piano/cello score (Martenot) is mixed in and eventually this takes over from the voices. This mix of sounds supports the dance's structure which shifts from informal improvisation into more formal motif accumulative device.

Task 3

Use the words of the poem below to make a sound collage which has a clear rhythmical feel.

Around the corner
Where to next?
Hanging loose,

Hanging out,
Up to scratch.

Where to next?
Down and out,
Ups and downs,
Uptight out of sight.

Where to next?
In leaps and bounds
In full swing,
Up, up and away.

By repeating certain words many times and adding pauses you can create driving rhythms like a rap, which you may record as accompaniment or speak live during the dance. The sounds and rhythms of the words will be most important in finding movement, but sometimes you may use the meaning of the words too.

Movement Sounds

Stamping feet, clapping hands, clicking fingers, softly rubbing palms together. In tap dance, Bharatha Natyam and Flamenco the rhythm of the feet are a crucial part of the whole dance form. In Flamenco the hands are also used with the help of the castanets to accent and reinforce the rhythms. The ankle bells of the Bharatha Natyam and Morris dancers add to the aural setting, so that the audience see and hear the rhythms.

Angika (Mayuri Boonham and Subathra Subramanian) explore Baratha Natyam to expand its possibilities for a duet relationship. Their *The-Triple-Hymn*, (2000), uses the traditional stamping to add percussive quality to the dynamic and rhythmic ranges. It contrasts to the sustainment of the soprano voice. The dance ends with blackout but the stamping can still be heard in the darkness.

Christopher Bruce's *Swansong* was a sequel to his *Ghost Dances* and continued Bruce's concern for the plight of political prisoners and oppressed people. The electro-acoustic score, written by Philip Chambon, has silent sections which allow us to hear the feet taps, hand claps, finger clicks and cane tapping conversations. These make an effective question and answer interrogation. The music-hall act by the guards is only a veneer for what is really black comedy and a sinister scene of torture.

Task 4

Create a solo dance in which the only accompaniment is from your body, (a mix of breath, your voice, your hands, feet etc). Be aware of any rhythms you may create and the overall form of the dance.

SILENCE

The rhythm of the dance can be kept only in the body and so all the content, form and style relies solely on the movement. All kinds of styles can be successful: comic or serious, dramatic or lyrical. Sometimes a dance may have started with a piece of music as accompaniment but will actually benefit from being performed without it, or to another piece of music entirely.

Silence may be chosen for certain sections of a dance, or at the start or end. In Martha Graham's *Primitive Mysteries* (1931) the main dramatic rituals occur in the silent sections and this intensifies their power.

Mary Wigman in her Expressionistic style composed many of her early works in silence in the early 1900s. She pioneered a new dance form called 'Absolute Dance' and her works ranged from the gentle to the dark and sinister. Her style was strongly emotional, no doubt influenced by Rudolf Laban and Isadora Duncan. In 1914 her *Witch Dance* used strange body shapes and clawing hands to express evil and mystery.

In a very different style of modern dance Richard Alston's *Soda Lake* is 'pure' movement. The content of the dance is a mix of the vast American desert landscape with the visual art concern for line, shape, volume and dimension. The highly abstract style and the empty, still environment make Alston's choice of silence as accompaniment highly appropriate.

Task 5

In a group of five, compose together a dance in silence called 'Echoes'. Be aware of the different sorts of canons that you may find. Be alert to how you design the movement in space with regard to direction, level, facings, exits and entrances, large and small size.

MUSIC – CHOOSING AND USING

A piece of music may well inspire you to leap to your feet in the privacy of your bedroom. The trap that you may fall into is that of allowing the music to dominate the movement. Music provides a pulse, a driving force and it can be a strong stimulus.

Choosing the music can happen at different times during the process of making a dance:

- dance and music composed simultaneously;

- dance created first and music created for it later;

- composed music with dance choreographed to it;

- dance and music created separately and performed for the first time together in performance (as seen in the work of Cunningham and Cage);

- a piece of suitable music is found for the dance while it is still in sketch form. In this way the dance may be shaped to suit the musical structure without the music totally dominating the movement.

Check List when Choosing Music

1. *Beware the Top Ten, old favourites and famous classics.* Often the lyrics or the audience's own strong feelings and connections are obstacles which may cloud the ideas which you are trying to express.
2. *Don't chop it or cut it!* It is inartistic to cut and rearrange someone else's music – it is also illegal. How would you like someone to rearrange your dance, or decide that they didn't need the middle bit and so throw it away?

3. *Quality.* Try to choose music which will not be scratched or sound as if it is being played underwater.

4. *Suitable balance.* A solo to a full symphony orchestra will not be easy. Consider the texture of the sound so that it is appropriate to the number of dancers and choice of images.

5. *Copyright.* There are laws which cover the use of music for performance; consider whether they might apply to you.

6. *Using pre-recorded music.* Take time to analyse its structure, tempo, metre, arrangement and instrumentation. Improvise to it and only when the music is clear to you can you be sure that it will not dictate the dance.

7. *In an ideal world* we would all dance to live music. Do you know a young musician or singer who may be interested in a bit of collaboration?

Task 6

In pairs create a 12 count phrase of movement and take turns in performing it to the following accompaniments:

- silence
- a piece of electronic music
- percussion instruments
- opera
- Irish music
- Radio 4

As you move speak the words which describe what you are doing, eg the counts, the actions, the quality etc.

Discuss the final results. How did the various accompaniments affect the movement?

The way you choose and work with accompaniment for your dances can help to make them more successful if you do not limit your choice to only one or two types of music or sound. Try to experiment by mixing, say, silence with music, or any of the different sorts of accompaniment together. Often music which makes good bathtime singing is best kept for the bubbles!

It is a good idea to listen properly to the music first and try to understand its tempo, metre etc. Make sure you are able to count it in a way which helps you to move with it. This may not be the way that the musician would count it, but it *will* help you to use the structure of the music in an imaginative way so that the dance is enhanced rather than restricted.

An interesting way of using metred music is to count it in different measures from that in which it is played. For example:

Music: 4-4-4-4-4-4 $= 24 \ (4 \times 6)$

Dance: 7 – 9 – 8 $= 24 \ (7 + 9 + 8)$

This kind of imaginative counting makes the use of chart music more possible, because you are not allowing the rigid beat to limit your movement. The music of Igor Stravinsky caused problems in terms of counting when Vaslav Nijinsky choreographed *Le Sacré du Printemps* in 1913. Stravinsky was experimenting in a revolutionary way with rhythm to produce a new style of music. This was rather like the explorations of the painter Picasso who, at the time, found inspiration in the forms of African sculpture. Stravinsky made new use of strong accents and complex *polyrhythms* (as heard in African music). In the dance, too, Nijinsky shocked the ballet world, using heaviness and aggression and by using turn-in of the legs rather than the usual elegant light turn-out. In one section of *Le Sacré du Printemps* the young people of a pagan Russian community stamp out the offbeat accents of the music. The asymmetry and counterpoint of group movement on top of the steady 4/4 metre express the raw energy of pagan ritual.

Task 7

Choose a piece of music that is short and has a simple clear structure. Make sure you understand the structure. Choose a piece of country and western music, a gospel song or from the Blues. Some classical works, for example by Bach or Handel, may also be useful. Write down or draw the music in your own way and then put your own movement ideas alongside. For example, an opening melody in the music may make you think of large curving runs, fast jumps or collapses, whereas the next section may be more suited to long stillnesses and sustained isolated gestures.

Paying attention to the appropriate use of motif repetition, development and variation, to contrast, transition and climax makes the score into a complete dance.

Musical Style

The music should respond to and complement the style of dance. The music may be lyrical, comic, dramatic style. A score which uses electronic sounds may be an abstract style and would need suitably abstract, 'pure' dance to complement it.

Traditional African music, played live on stage, leads the movement rhythms in *So What!* by Badejo Arts. Celebration of life is clearly expressed through the shared rhythms and dynamic phrasing. The choice of traditional music style by Christopher Bruce suits his use of folk dance steps and people-related issues. Whereas Siobhan Davies's 'pure' dance is suited to her choice of contemporary music, such as the percussive, complex rhythms of Kevin Volans. Shobana Jeyasingh's *Fine Frenzy* (1999) is rhythmically intricate too and the choice of a Django Bates's jazz score (played live) complements the style and theme of the dance. It mixes music from different cultures with everyday sounds such as sirens, drilling and peals of bells into the saxophone quartet. Together the dance and music create the atmosphere of a busy London suburb.

Matthew Bourne's use of original ballet scores supports his narrative style, because the music was written to tell stories. Composers Drosten Madden and Steve Blake write jazz-based mixes of popular music styles, such as rock, pop and easy listening, with sound effects and film tracks providing Lea Anderson with a diverse, catchy and appealing sound. It is a suitable lively, fresh, often loud setting for the quirky repetitive rhythms of her movement style.

Task 8

Research on the internet or in a music shop to find a piece of music which mixes different cultures or styles. Make a dance (solo or group) which responds to the music with its styles of movement.

THE RELATIONSHIP OF DANCE TO MUSIC

As we see in the previous example of Fokine's *Le Sacré du Printemps* the dance can set its own rhythms and accents to counterpoint the music. In other words the dance does not have to do exactly what the music 'tells' it to. Choreographers have different preferences for how they relate their dances to music.These different styles range from following the music note for note, to not even listening to it! The different relationships of dance to music are:

- *direct correlation;*
- *visualisation;*
- *emphasise mood, character or narrative;*
- *mutual co-existence;*
- *disassociation.*

Direct Correlation

Changes in the music's pitch, key, dynamics or tempo will be matched by the dance. The styles of both Mark Morris and George Balanchine use musicality as a mainspring of their work. Balanchine's *Agon* (1957) is supported by the steady pulse of Stravinsky's music, but the dancers play around in a jazzy way with time and rhythm in the same way as the instruments of the orchestra. Balanchine and Stravinsky once described their work as *hearing* the dance and *seeing* the music.

There is a canon of jumps for the flowers in the *Waltz of the Flowers* section of Mark Morris's *The Hard Nut*. It follows note for note the Tchaikovsky music and cascades delightfully with life and energy.

Visualisation

With his English style of classical ballet Sir Frederick Ashton was noted for his musicality. His dancing was noted for its complex and musical rhythms. In *The Dream* he used the music's rhythms in different ways to show the contrast of the fairies to the human characters. The fairy jumps are timed to be in the air on the downbeat. In contrast the humans dance on the beat. In another section, as the Mendelssohn *Wedding March* plays, the reconciled couples make church-like arches for each other to walk under, an appropriate visualisation of the image.

Task 9

In a group of between three and five dancers use *music visualisation* to match the dance to changes in the music, eg changes of level match changes of key or changes of tempo, are matched.
OR
Take a theme for a dance such as: a journey; African village life; rush hour, and research to find a piece of music which will enhance mood and narrative. Compose a dance which uses the music appropriately.

Emphasise Mood, Character or Narrative

In Fokine's expressive and romantic style ballet, *Petrouchka*, the music supports the characters, story, psychological meanings and atmosphere in its variety of rhythms and orchestration. *Orchestration* is how different musical instruments or voices are blended, each has its own *timbre*, or tone colour, eg a tuba is unlike a violin. The composer Stravinsky chose a piano to represent the puppet in conflict with the rest of the orchestra, that is the other characters. The piano played the puppet's inner pain. There are also sections of music based on Russian folk tunes and dances for the people and atmosphere of the fair.

Similarly in Sir Frederick Ashton's *Tales of Beatrix Potter* (1970, an EMI Films picture), the John Lanchbery score has a musical theme for each animal character – a waltz for mice, a march for pigs, a polka for Jeremy Fisher and a tarantella for Peter Rabbit. Other music carries the story and the themes are woven into it.

Mutual Co-existence

When the dance holds its own identity strongly alongside the music the two exist together but do not necessarily match. Lea Anderson works with music in this way. In a review of *The Big Dance Number* we are told:

'. . . it's enough to demonstrate Anderson's ready understanding of rhythm, the energy of an irregular pattern, the tension of racing or crossing the music. How she can enliven the plodding insistent beat of the Drostan Madden/Steve Blake musical styles that she favours.'

Stephanie Jordan[1]

Both Richard Alston and Shobana Jeyasingh work with music in this way too. The dance has a kind of conversation with the music. In Alston's *Strong Language* (1987), the music is on an 8 count but the dance is counted 3-3-2. This heightens the energy and freshens the overall look. Alston comments:

'body rhythms are different from musical rhythms . . . Instead of having a regular musical shape my pieces had an asymmetrical phrasing rather like speech.'[2]

At one point in Jeyasingh's videodance *Duets with Automobiles* (1994) the dancers answer the call of intricate chanting. A call and response relationship with music is often used in African and Indian genres. An African master drummer plays the signals telling the dancers when to change steps. A delightful use of this is seen in the third section of Badejo Arts' *So What!* Musician Peter Badejo calls, in Yuroba language, and the other musicians respond verbally whilst dancer, Francis Angol, answers physically. It is a witty play with the rhythm, pitch of voice, language and the physical replies.

Disassociation

This is the extreme end of the relationship of dance and music, they act totally independently of one another. Typical of this is the work of Merce Cunningham and composer John Cage. Often the dancers would not have ever heard the music until the first night when they found themselves dancing to it. Siobhan Davies's early work involved making dance before hearing the score and so she worked independently of the music's timing.

Perhaps by the end of this chapter you will feel more adventurous to try to work with different types of accompaniment or with a style of one

---

[1] *The Cholmondeleys Spring 1988*, in *Dance Theatre Journal*, 6.2 1988, p. 27.
[2] In *Making a Ballet*, C. Crisp and M. Clarke, Macmillan, 1974, p. 81.

of the choreographers who are described. Take some time to have a bit of fun and experiment with something new.

6.1 FEET FIRST, *choreography Linda Ashley*

REFERENCES

Further Reading

Jordan, Stephanie *Moving Music. Dialogues with Music in Twentieth Century Ballet* (2000), Dance Books.

Teck, Katherine, *Ear Training for the Body. A Dancer's Guide* (1994), Princeton Book Co.
Twiner, Antony *The Muncey Music Book* (1986), Dance Books.

Video and DVD

From The Video Place: www.theplace.org.uk On *Spring Re-Loaded 6; The-Triple-Hymn*, Angika. *Time Lapses*, Rosemary Lee peels back the layers that make a dance. On *Spring Re-Loaded 5; Fine Frenzy*, Shobana Jeyasingh.
Available from www.dancebooks.co.uk *The Tales of Beatrix Potter*, Frederick Ashton.

Music

Task 7 – Bach, *Little Fugue in G minor.*
Handel, *Trio Sonata in A major Op. 5.*
From *Springsound; Gypsy Trail* or *Café Jive.*
Task 8 – From *Springsound; Driving Soft Rock.*
Task 9 – From *Springsound; Funkoid.* From *Dance!; Level Headed; Africa Calling; Moa Hunters; Commuting.* From *New Zealand Music for Creative Dance; Trains; Rainmaker.*

Web Sites

Dance music from:
www.surreydancemusic.co.uk
www.ucamusic.com
www.pastperfect.com
www.badejoarts.co.uk
www.danz.org.nz

Chapter 7

EXTRAS AND ESSENTIALS

PROPS, MASKS, COSTUMES, SET AND LIGHTING

When choosing these bear in mind that they must be a *necessary* part of the dance. They should emphasise the images, illusions and design.

> 'I used masks and props – the masks to have the dancer become something else; the props to extend the physical size in space (as extra bones and flesh).'
>
> *Alwin Nikolais*[1]

Some examples of the use of props, masks, set, costume and lighting in dance are:

- *The Green Table* (1932) by Kurt Jooss, where a green baize snooker table represents the immovable political differences and war games that explode around it. It also gives opportunity for rich development of level in the power struggle. All the dancers wore masks which resembled ageing politicians plotting war.
- *Ghost Dances* by Christopher Bruce. Here the death masks of the oppressors combined with the body painting emphasise their primitive, sinewy movement and their sinister presence.
- *Go Las Vegas* (1995). Lea Anderson chose a novel idea of handing out torches to the audience and at a given signal they switched them on, lighting the Featherstonehaughs' phosphorescent silver suits. The dancers' hands and faces remained black so the suits seemed to dance with a life of their own. A fine example of how costume and light design enhanced the theme of the dance, that is the faceless glamour of show biz.

---

[1] *Vision of Modern Dance*, p. 114.

7.1 NINE SONGS *(1993), Cloud Gate Dance Theatre of Taiwan, choreography Lin Hwai-min; dancer Huang Shu-hui; masks Lin Shu-feng and Wang Yao-chun; costumes Lin Hwai-min and Lo Ruey-chi; set Ming Cho Lee*

Props

These can easily inspire dance because there are so many ways in which they can cause movement to happen. In the magical world of theatre a newspaper can be anything you wish it to be. You can pick it up to sweep the floor, cloak someone in it, roll it up and look through it, sit on it, stand on it. It can be smooth, spiky. You could even read it!

It may be the colour or feel or shape of the prop that gives you ideas for movement. Sometimes it may be how the object itself moves – the roll of an egg, the unfolding of a plastic bag. The property itself may take on a meaning or meanings in dramatic sitūations, for example a net tutu may become the leaves of a tree or a tennis racquet become prison bars.

If dancers are to use props they should be safe to handle, although watching Wim Vandekeybus's dancers throw and catch bricks at

7.2 *THE GREEN TABLE* *(1932), choreography Kurt Jooss*

terrifying speed makes one wonder (*Roseland,* 1990). In contrast he also uses the lightness of a falling feather, playfully kept in the air by two dancers' breath. This gives a real sense of the weight of things and of the pull of gravity.

Props can certainly add to realistic images. Lea Anderson's use of books, playing cards, magazines, big rubber tyres, suitcases and camping gear combine well with the two sets of characters in *Cross Channel.* A fun, holiday atmosphere is the result.

Sometimes a costume can become a prop. In *Boy* the boiler suit becomes a kite, an invisible sparring partner and a bathing suit needing to be dried. This all adds to the collage structure showing the viewer the many ideas associated with the boy's day on the beach.

Imaginative use of props in Christopher Bruce's *Swansong* sees the chair and canes used to depict images of torture, weapons, shields and imprisonment.

The following is a suggested list of properties which you may wish to try:

chairs	rope	boxes	walking stick
elastic	feathers	bucket	paper bags
hoop	ladder	balloons	scarves
fabric	umbrella	broom	traffic cones
plastic flowers		lampshades	frying pan

Task 1

Collect a number of unrelated objects and then choose one of the Shakespeare plays, eg *A Midsummer Night's Dream*. Try to identify the main characters and the general plot (not too much detail). In *A Midsummer Night's Dream* there are some strong characters such as Oberon, Titania (King and Queen of the fairies), Puck, the lovers, Bottom and the fairy chorus. There is a general feeling of magic and mischief! Use the props with the characters to rewrite a short version of the story for your dance narrative structure.

Masks

Masks have had a powerful influence on ritual dance and theatre since primitive times. They have been made of many different materials: wood, stone, metal, fibre, bone, clay, cloth, plants, feathers and many more. Whatever materials are easily to hand will be used to weave the magic spell and make the mask special in style to suit the dance.

In many parts of the world ritual dance has strong symbolic powers. For instance in Bali the *barong* is a monster who fights an evil monster, therefore exorcising evil from the community and warding off bad luck or illness. The *barong* consists of two dancers underneath a fantastic costume and mask.

Often the wearer of the mask is regarded as sacred or supernatural and the mask becomes holy, to be touched only by the special few. The mask gives the wearer a new identity, a god of nature or a spirit, often releasing inhibitions. In Mali, Africa, a ritual mask dance is used to honour the death of their village dignitaries. Up to a week long the ritual establishes order and balance, pacifying the spirit of the dead. The masks can be up to sixteen feet high and are blade shaped. The dancers sweep the ground with the top of the mask in the ceremony, symbolically cleansing the ground.

Involving masks can be a challenging way of making dances. Masks can be made out of a simple brown paper-bag design, full and half head, nose and eyes only. They can be extremely intricately decorated with beads, sequins, plants, fabric or a simple copy of your own face in a certain mood. The list of characters and moods is endless.

Animals are frequently a feature of dance and masks have been used by various choreographers to add a sense of realism. David Bintley's '*Still Life*' *at the Penguin Café* (1988) has many delightful masks designed by Hayley Griffin. They range from a striking, stripey zebra with the finishing touch of the mane on top to the realistic Brazilian Woolly Monkey and the cartoon-like Great Auk. Masks for Frederick Ashton's *Tales of Beatrix Potter* were designed by Rostislav Doboujinsky. They are surprisingly lifelike and true to the illustrations of the original story.

French choreographer Maguy Marin dressed all her dancers in masks to look like nineteenth century dolls in her *Cinderella* (1985). This emphasised the dark and dreamlike atmosphere of her retelling of the fairy tale. Another French choreographer, Philippe Decouflé, uses masks to create an *X-Files* type world which is scary and comic at the same time. He has choreographed music videos for bands such as Fine Young Cannibals and New Order and for the opening and closing ceremonies for the 1992 Winter Olympics. His stagework *Codex* (1986) was witty and surreal in style, full of illusion. Froggy-fishy-reptilian dancers wore masks that joined onto the all-in-one stripey body clinging wet suits. The face mask was asymmetrically striped and patched to distort the human face. Their antics, running around wearing gigantic flippers on their feet, bring a smile to the face and we are unsure as to whether it can be real or just a dream.

Task 2

Using the signs of the Zodiac, create masks for the various symbols of the people in your group. Improvise around the personal characteristics of the signs, eg Capricorn is patient. Choreograph a dance that explores how they may react to each other.

Costumes

As with masks, what a dancer wears, whether simple black or lavish *Kathakali* costume, is to be regarded as an extension of the body. The simplest costume can be effective if appropriate to the range and mood of the movement. For instance, a lyrical style dance may well be best suited to light chiffon or silk. (See illustration 7.3 *Five Brahms Waltzes in the Manner of Isadora Duncan*). As we see in the photo the fabric of the costume also becomes a prop, enhancing the flow and dynamics of the movement.

Of course dancing in pillowcases, hats, towels or wellington boots will suggest a more comic style. Sometimes, as in South African dance, wellington boots can become the sound accompaniment by slapping and stamping. Merce Cunningham created a dance based around an oversize sweater which had no hole for the head but four sleeves!

Costumes and masks should work together to express the theme of a dance. Although some of the animal masks of *'Still Life' at the Penguin Café* are realistic they are given human qualities by some of the costumes, such as the Great Auks dressed as waiters and the cowboy dungarees of the Texan Kangaroo Rat. Bintley's concern for endangered species, who are featured in this dance, is clear when we see materials from animal costumes worn by models on the catwalk. This could be interpreted as a criticism of the fur trade, or indeed of any trade which uses animal parts for human decoration.

Something as seemingly simple as footwear can have an enormous expressive impact. The romance of eighteenth-century ballet was emphasised by the innovation of a dance shoe without a heel. This facilitated *toe dancing* which was later to be further developed into the blocked *pointe* shoe. This allowed faster multiple turning and of course the look of floating above the ground.

Hans van Manen's choice of high heels in *Piano Variations* affects the women's posture and adds height, expressing 'attitude', power and control. At one point they stamp and seem to be trampling the solo male under their heels. Rather than increasing power the absurd idea of attaching a large board to one foot, in Decouflé's *Codex*, has the effect of disabling one dancer. Whenever he tries to walk he has to overcome a handicap. Added to which his costume of hip waders, normally designed to keep out water, keep filling up *with* water! This is a mixed up, muddled up, shook up Decouflé world and no mistake. A similar distorted planet is where Maguy Marin's *Groosland* (1989) is set. Her dancers wear padded suits to make them appear very overweight and assist her satire of the sylphs of the world of ballet. Not a million miles away are the costumes used by Lea Anderson (designer Sandy Powell) for her *Out on the Windy Beach* (1998). As reported in a newspaper review:

> **'Perhaps the man who ambled drunkenly up to the raised stage at Brighton's Hove Lawns thought he was suffering from a particularly bad bout of delirium tremens when he saw six fluorescent-yellow creatures with goggles and flip-flops.'**
>
> *Nadine Meisner*[2]

Together the costume's colour and the protective-style clothing worn support the theme of concern about pollution in the oceans and loss of the ozone layer over earth's skies. At one point skin is revealed only to reveal melanoma-like skin tattoos.

Sometimes costumes are chosen that are not only effective in their simplicity but also may be inexpensive. Cunningham's dancers and Alston's solo *Soda Lake* wear simple all-in-one, figure hugging garments to show the lines of the body clearly.

Sometimes just colour theme and pattern can work, as in Siobhan Davies's *White Man Sleeps,* where the costumes' colours and stripes tone perfectly with the dance floor and lighting effects.

Costume in some styles of dance is chosen to give authenticity, as in Adzido Pan African Dance Ensemble's *Under African Skies.* The narrative takes a journey from the west to the east and the south of the African continent and, as the dances reveal varying regional styles, so do the costumes.

Choreographers throughout history have used costume designs which extend and strengthen the dance content. Whether it be the illusion of a traditional tutu of the classical dancer hovering lightly above the floor or the everyday look of the post modern dancers as they perform on roof-tops, their costume helps us to know more about the style or the significance of a dance.

---

[2] *Maritime Disaster* in *The Sunday Times* 31 May 1998.

7.3 *FIVE BRAHMS WALTZES IN THE MANNER OF ISADORA DUNCAN (1976),*
choreography Frederick Ashton, for Ballet Rambert, dancer Lucy Burge

Set

From the fifteenth century onwards the beginnings of ballet as court entertainment always used the finest artists to design the scenery. Italy, France and England produced huge, splendid backdrops of realistic proportion and perspective.

Set may be designed to create illusion and atmosphere. In the Renaissance, dancers floated on clouds with the use of flying machinery. By the late 1790s the engineer Liparotti was using counterweighted wires to fly and balance individual dancers. This allowed dancers to remain on their tip toes for longer and was an important influence on the growth of *pointe* dancing. Later the blocked toe shoe allowed dancers to work on *pointe* without the wires and the Romantic Ballet gained enormous expressive impact from this technological innovation.

In the nineteenth century the Romantic movement had a more realistic look such as you might see in Ciceri's *Giselle*. Later when Romantic Ballet developed, larger spectacles laid the foundation of a new approach to stage design.

Serge Diaghilev, an entrepreneur deeply committed to the work of visual artists such as Benois and Bakst, became interested in ballet and

7.4 SWANSONG *(1987), choreographer Christopher Bruce, dancer Koen Onzia, photographer Bill Cooper*

founded the Ballets Russes. He insisted on designer and choreographer working closely together. Benois designed for *Les Sylphides* and *Petrouchka* and Bakst for *The Firebird* and *L'Après Midi d'un Faune*.

Their lavish, exotic and highly colourful sets and costumes perfectly matched the ground breaking content and movement of the ballets.

Later in the twentieth century Martha Graham's less narrative style needed abstract set and costume, she worked with Japanese designer Isamu Noguchi. This collaboration changed the look of stage design. His sparse, free-standing sculptural sets were integral to the dance. For example in *Frontier*, Noguchi's first work for Graham, the solo is set on a section of fence. Two ropes fly away diagonally upwards from each side of the fence. The dance of this lone female pioneer is set in the vast space of American frontier lands. The dance reaches out in all directions from the territory of the fence, as does the set. Noguchi's design supports the emotional meaning of the dance, and the landscape in which the woman dances.

Later Merce Cunningham saw design as a completely different element. He saw dance, music and set as separate on stage and therefore broke the conventions of centuries. He collaborated with artists like Andy Warhol, Robert Rauschenberg and Jasper Johns. In *Rainforest* (1968) the dancers moved with, around and in spite of Warhol's helium-filled silver pillows.

Matthew Bourne's West End productions such as *Swan Lake* and *Cinderella* have had lavish set designs by Lez Brotherston. The Prince's bed is bigger than ever one could imagine and it has multi functions. Turned around it becomes the palace balcony to hold the waving Royal Family. Later a flock of swans enter from underneath it. The realistic explosion of the ballroom in *Cinderella* is a cleverly designed illusion. Accompanied by earsplitting bangs and blinding flashes the set is blown apart before our eyes.

Set can emphasise important abstract meanings of a dance. Lin Hwai-min's *Nine Songs* reflects the cycle of the seasons. The set uses the Chinese symbol of death and rebirth, the lotus flower, as its main image. There is an actual lotus pond at the front of the stage and the whole set is an enlarged lotus painting. The dance's content combines ancient Chinese gods and imagery with more recent political events. If you look at the photo at the start of this chapter you will see how the various designers collaborated to juxtapose traditional and modern.

The backdrop (Madelaine Morris) for Shobana Jeyasingh's *Memory and Other Props* is lit (Judy Carter) in different ways, changing its significance to suit the dance's meaning. Sometimes the backdrop is a wired glittering brain, then it is the past as the dancers are placed behind the gauze, like shadows or dim memories.

Tables, chairs, curtains, ladders, boxes, ropes, bicycles, mobiles, scaffold, rubber-plants, planks of wood, all these give a richness of level and dimension to the dance.

Richard Alston's *Wildlife* uses huge mobiles designed by Richard Smith. The dancers move around, under and through them, always echoing the sharp edges of the set, which itself moves by the use of electric motors. It turns and flies up and down. The music too, by Nigel Osborne, is influenced by the set until finally all the elements come together in a flat, zig-zag energy.

Set design in the work of Pina Bausch can be startling. Dancers move on floors covered with dead leaves (*Bluebeard*, 1977) or mud (*Le Sacré du Printemps*, 1975), or ankle deep in pink and white flowers (*Carnations*, 1975). Her works of despair and terror are shocking and real. Dancers hurl themselves towards each other over and over again in hostile, surreal surroundings.

Sometimes the set may become so much a hands-on part of the dance it could be called a prop-set. The large ladder used in Robert Cohan's *Hunter of Angels* is the only set on a bare stage, but it is manipulated by the dancers who need all their physical strength and skill in order to move it safely and expressively. It becomes a labyrinth, angel's wings, a womb and Jacob's Ladder to heaven. Similarly the set (Simon Dorman and Oblique) for *Faking It* (Motionhouse, 1997) is designed to provide an adventure playground which physically challenges the dancers. It is constructed from large boards and various structures which the dancers climb up, hang off and precariously balance on. Illusions of dancers flying and floating are enhanced by the lighting (Mark Parry). Both these sets also add extra high and low level possibilities into the movement. This could be achieved just as well with simple rostra.

Traditional set is replaced when dance is removed to outdoor locations. Site-specific work is very common these days. Lea Anderson's videodance *Cross Channel* is set on location between London and Calais. It uses various settings: roads, railway, Channel ferry, beaches, cliff tops, tents, to present us with almost a snapshot album of the holiday.

Interestingly enough the costumes here sometimes match the setting, like the cyclists' clothes, but at other times are from another era. Together the female dancers' 1950s bathing costumes, dresses, hats and 1920s feather boas with the men's 1960s Hawaiian shirts create a kind of time warp and add interest beyond a simple realistic style.

Sometimes the risk involved with the weather in site-specific work can create problems as well as interest. Anderson's *Out on the Windy Beach* seemed to tempt fate because the wind *really* blew around the specially designed beach hut and its wooden jetty! Another unforeseen for out of of doors performance may be the wandering audience, one of whom (rather worse for drink) stumbled onto the stage on Brighton beach. Crowd control may be a health and safety consideration.

Another choreographer who uses locations is Shobana Jeyasingh. Videodance *Duets with Automobiles* uses a variety of modern interiors in London. The dances echo and express the architectural features such as corridors and circular mezzanine floors. This is typical of her dance style mixing traditional and modern to express, not characters of the gods and stories, but explorations of geometry, time and space. Seeking permission to film on location is an important consideration.

The setting of videodance *Downstairs* (1995, Maria Voortman and Roberto de Jonge) *is* the dance. It explores an incongruous pairing of descending stairs wearing *pointe* shoes, taking the balletic convention of balance to risky extremes. Rather than emphasising the perfect holding of balance on pointe it focuses on the precarious dangers of falling. Dancers hurtle down the stairs, they wobble, totter and jump from one stair to the next and we sense their fear.

Task 3

Build a structure from any objects available. As a group, discuss what kind of place this might be: a city street, another planet, a house etc. Find suitable characters to inhabit the set and appropriate costumes and props for them. Improvise together, emphasising the imaginative use of the various objects.

Props, masks, set and costume should grow from the needs of the dance, not be added extras. It is a good idea to keep an eye out in charity shops for any interesting items that may be useful one day.

Lighting

Human beings are sensitive to changes of light. It affects our mood. Seasonal affected disorder (SAD), which some people suffer during winter when the days grow shorter, is a good example of this. Lighting design in dance exploits this and holds many possibilities to emphasise meaning and create illusion. It can vary in direction and brightness. These should be appropriate to the dancer's placement on the stage and to the mood or meaning. Often for dance side lighting is used because it gives a clearer view of the dancers' bodies.

Here is a list of some technical terms for lighting:

- *General wash* – this is the overall way that light 'paints' the whole stage.

- *Spot lights* – highlight specific areas of the stage, perhaps to draw attention to a prop or a specific dancer. They can vary in size and in sharpness.

- *Gels* – are placed in front of lights to change the colour. Obviously colour influences mood. Also they should be sympathetic to the colour of the costumes.

- *Cyclorama* – is a light-coloured backdrop which may be varied in colour by shining different lights onto it.

- *Gobos* – are cut-out patterned cards placed in front of lights to throw patterns, such as leafy forests or swirls, onto the stage.

Dancers can encounter problems with lights blinding them as they dance and, although they can be trained to deal with this, it is an important safety consideration. Safe placement of wires and the lights is important too. Similarly flashing disco lights, strobes and glitter balls can have great effects but need to be used with appropriate safety.

One of the earliest lighting innovations influenced the success and growth of Romantic Ballet in the nineteenth century. Similar to the *pointe* shoe, tutu and flying machinery, gas-light (ether) was new to dance theatre. For the first time the auditorium lights went out and only the stage was lit. Ballerinas danced in 'ghostly moonlight'. Light, delicate sylphs danced on their toes and 'flew'. The audience must have been captivated by the new ethereal illusion.

7.5 *NINE SONGS (1993), Cloudgate Dance Theatre of Taiwan, choreography Lin Hwai-min, lighting Lin Keh-hua*

There are many examples of successful lighting design which enhance the movement and meaning of a dance. Lin Hwai-min for Cloud Gate Dance Theatre of Taiwan used a river of candles in the final section of *Nine Songs* (lighting design Lin Keh-hua). The effect was stunning as the dance drew to its climax. The choreographer explains that the river he has lived next to for many years has influenced his life and that this was part of the theme of the dance. Clearly the fire-safety regulations would need consideration.

Here a dance critic draws clear connections between light, set and costumes so that we see how the physical setting of a dance should work as a whole:

> 'The setting is a quaintly romanticised African landscape. The lighting plot is packed with dramatic transformations; authentic costumes from differing cultures are thrown into juxtaposition and tricked out with the likes of dapper white patent leather shoes . . .'
> David Henshaw[3]

---

[3] *Black Attitudes*, in *Dance Theatre Journal*. 8,4, Spring 1991.

The lighting and physical setting work as a coherent whole in Siobhan Davies's *White Man Sleeps*. Designers David Buckland (set) and Peter Mumford (lighting) collaborate to light the painted striped dance floor, blocking rectangular patterns. This complements the bands of colour on the figure hugging costumes and the music (composer Kevin Volans) which has a sharp, edgy, percussive feel. Lighting is used particularly effectively to brighten in the livelier sections. At one point a solo dancer lies in stillness lit in a bright rectangle whilst around her a duet is danced in dimmer light. The stillness is strengthened by the spot light.

In Christopher Bruce's *Swansong* David Mohr's design plays a major part in the meaning of the dance. It lights a bare stage (prison cell) and emphasises moments when the prisoner is alone by the lit window high upstage left. He is drawn towards it longing for freedom. At the end of the dance he travels along a diagonal shaft of light towards the window in a symbolic final flight to freedom. The tragedy is that behind him the guards are left in their opening stillness and seem to be looking at the victim's corpse.

Lighting can emphasise atmosphere and energy levels of a dance. This is seen in Shobana Jeyasingh's *Fine Frenzy* (1999), the backdrop is hung

7.6 TWISTED *(1999), Motionhouse Dance Company, choreography*
Kevin Finnan, Louise Richards, dancer Lisi Perry

7.7 Shobana Jeyasingh Dance Company 1998

with energetic wire sculptures and some of them are lit with strips of flashing light. Projections of film evoke the rush of speeding traffic. Throughout, the colour and brightness fluctuate in response to the dance and the music. Together the physical setting and movement place the viewer in the hustle and bustle of a busy London high street.

Task 4

From the photos 7.1, 7.6 and 7.7 describe how you think the costume, set and lights may enhance the style of the dance. What do these components tell you about the dance content or meaning? To find out more about these dance companies and their styles research on the internet or in this book.

PHYSICAL SETTING – A FINAL WORD

It is clear that props, masks, costume, set and lighting should all work together to support the content, style and images of the dance. This can be as simple as the costuming, white light and clean lines of the sculpture in *Soda Lake* (Richard Alston) or as complex and lavish as the sets for Matthew Bourne's *Cinderella*. The crucial factor for success is that the physical setting enhances the dance style and meaning.

Sometimes the removal of set and light can achieve as interesting effect as the presence. *Time Lapses* (Sue Maclennan and Rosemary Lee) is a piece which has an overall pre-set form but includes improvisation during performance. As the dance progresses the working light and the accompaniment of the performers' voices are replaced gradually with with more theatrical lighting (Aidee Malone), and an electronic score (MacDonald and Vargo/Martinau). This corresponds to the choreography's increasing theatricality and formal structure. Motifs become more repeated and defined. The whole performance is like seeing the process of composition (*finding, choosing, shaping*: see Chapter 8), which normally happens in the rehearsal studio. Suitably simple, informal costume (t-shirt and trousers) plus the set as the open stage (no wings and the use of the real stage back door as the only entry point), add the finishing touches to a dance studio atmosphere.

Safe and accurate placement of set, props and light is essential. Entrance and exit points need to be clear, or on occasion may even be expanded on, say by using blocks to hide dancers which they suddenly appear from. Costume colour, size, fabric, weight should allow comfortable, safe and appropriate movement for dancers. Of course this *may* include restricting movement for a desired effect as in *Codex*, when part of one dancer's costume is a strong bungy. The solo is about trying to cross the stage whilst the elastic pulls him back!

The collaboration required to achieve harmony between physical setting, dance, dancers and accompaniment needs teamwork and careful consideration. Philippe Decouflé has said that it can take up to two years to bring a large production to the stage! Working to deadlines is going to be important for you too. As you head towards a performance, or an exam, managing rehearsals and a time line is crucial. The next chapter is written to help you understand some of the skills and strategies which may be useful.

REFERENCES

Further Reading

Harrison, Mary Kent *How to Dress Dancers* (1998), Dance Books.
Cooper, Susan *Staging Dance* (1998), A & C Black.
Pallin, Gail *Stage Management, The Essential Handbook* (2000), Titan Books.
Docherty, Peter *Design for Performance, from Diaghilev to the Pet Shop Boys* (1996), Lund Humphries.

Video and DVD

Available from www.dancebooks.co.uk *Boy* and *Downstairs* on *The best of Springdance Cinema 96*. *Cinderella*, Frederick Ashton (recorded 1969). *Cinderella* and *Groosland*, Maguy Marin. *Gumboots, an explosion of spirit and song*. African Dance. *'Still Life' at the Penguin Café*, David Bintley. *The Tales of Beatrix Potter*, Frederick Ashton.
From The Video Place: www.theplace.org.uk *Fine Frenzy*, Shobana Jeyasingh. On *Spring Re-Loaded 4*.

Music

Tasks 1,2,3 – Any Balinese, Indian or Thai music which can help set a mood, flow and drama.
'World Service' by Man Jumping, EGED 49.
'Zoolook', Jean-Michel Jarre, Polydor POLH 15.
From *Springsound: Cruisy*.
From *New Zealand Music for Creative Dance: Mumbo Jumbo*, Gareth Farr.

Web sites

www.cloudgate.org.tw
www.motionhouse.com.uk

Chapter 8

FROM PROCESS TO PERFORMANCE

FINDING, CHOOSING, SHAPING

Throughout this book there are examples of choreographers' work and we can see that they make dances based on their personal choice of images, themes and stimuli. Often a choreographer has favourite themes, for instance Christopher Bruce often starts with ethical and political issues such as in *Swansong* and *Ghost Dances*. When composing dances you too will need to find stimuli or starting points that interest *you*. Then you will go through a problem-solving process of how to find physical images that express your chosen stimulus. Making a dance is like solving a physical puzzle.

This chapter will take you through the various stages of this process from the first explorations, into rehearsal and to performance. During this process you will be using information from the other chapters of the book to inform your choices. To help you further there are Key Skills signposted using the symbol ➤ so that you may track these as you work.

FINDING – STIMULUS, IMPROVISATION

'You are your own master and student. There is no value in copying what someone else has done. You must search within your own body. What you discover there will be for your own benefit.'

Hanya Holm[1]

While building your technical competence and understanding of dynamics, time and space you will often find yourself improvising, exploring movement, trying out new ideas, as in some of the earlier tasks. Your

---

[1] Hanya Holm, *Vision of Modern Dance*. p. 71.

imagination is a special source by which ideas are chosen, movements selected, and gives the final dance its own unique individual style.

Use stimuli which are of interest to you. Do you like poetry? Try to use a poem as a springboard for movement ideas. Do you keep a diary? Take a day from it and create movement from the events and feelings of that day. Do you have a strong belief in something? Can you express this in movement?

Such starting points or stimuli can be drawn from any aspect of life. They may be very clear, even from the start; begin as a vague hint or even change completely during improvisation. Sometimes the starting point can be the movement itself.

Paul Taylor said

'I don't know where ideas come from. If I waited for inspiration I'd never get anything done . . . I just get busy in the studio and sometimes when I start I haven't got a clue what we're going to do. I just start. If it doesn't lead anywhere, then I start over . . . There's no lack of ideas; it's harder to eliminate them and get what you want.'[2]

During improvisation you allow your body and mind to follow freely along an idea and try not to worry too much about technique. Try out things for the first time, be spontaneous. Eventually you will realise that there is as much skill in learning to improvise as there is in learning technique. Letting go is not always easy. Try to be totally involved with the stimulus and movement and this will help you to be less inhibited.

'Improvisations require different styles of thought at different moments in their evolution. A dialogue between wildness and order.'[3]

Improvisation has long been a strong influence in the world of theatre. In many ancient dance traditions, such as Indian dance and Flamenco, it is a much admired and respected skill. The dancers play with the

[2] Paul Taylor, *Quintet: 5 American Dance Companies* (1972), Maria Hodgson, Macmillan, New York, p. 72.
[3] Miranda Tufnell and Chris Crickmay, *Body, Space, Image* (1990), Virago Press. Introduction.

8.1 Isadora Duncan

intricate cross-rhythms which results in brilliant cascades of steps and sounds. Traditional western theatre tended to gradually discard improvisation in favour of more rigid rules of presentation. This is particularly noticeable in classical ballet, where the role of choreographer may be one of ultimate responsibility for choosing the dancers' movements. The work of Isadora Duncan, on the other hand, was based on freedom of choice of movement even *during* the performance. After several years of formal approaches such as those of Martha Graham, in the 1940s and 1950s Merce Cunningham and composer John Cage reintroduced improvisation as a main component of choreography.

In the 1960s this was developed still further in New York by such dancers as Steve Paxton, Douglas Dunn and Yvonne Rainer. They questioned every aspect of form to include improvisation in performance and audience participation and gradually it became popular not only to watch dance but also to join in. This approach is still being used today. You can see it in *Time Lapses* (Rosemary Lee, Sue Maclennan).

Improvisation is a way of finding new movement so that you are not always producing the same ideas. From whatever your stimulus is, try to react spontaneously to it and start to make choices from the fragments which you feel work best. You will need to concentrate deeply, as often movements which are successful are also instantly forgotten! Treat this not as a source of frustration, however, but rather one of fun and magic.

➤ Information technology

You may consider using a video camera to keep a rehearsal diary. By watching your improvisations after rehearsal you may see something that you had forgotten about, or a gesture that you hadn't realised was effective, or even movement that you didn't know you had created!

Task 1

➤ Problem Solving

Choose from the list of stimuli below and see how much different movement material you can think up in five minutes.

1. Electronic music
2. A wall of the studio
3. A piece of clothing

4. A photo
5. A stimulus of your own choice.

As part of your course you may keep a working diary or log book. Record descriptions of some of the movements that you found through improvisation and how they expressed the stimulus. Try to use accurate action, space, time and dynamics terms in your descriptions.

CHOOSING – ABSTRACTION, FORMING, STYLE

Gradually the movement material will begin to be more clearly shaped into phrases which have a beginning, middle and end. Like a sentence it starts to make sense, to have a kind of movement logic with an overall form and feeling.

You will find that phrases vary in length and this helps to create interest. They also reveal ideas, impressions and design which tell us more about the original stimulus. This is achieved by a process called *abstraction*.

Task 2

➤ Problem Solving, Information Technology

Watch an extract of dance on video from a favourite choreographer and make notes on:

- full title, choreographer, dancer/s, date of first performance;
- the stimulus and content;
- describe two motifs and how they use action, space, time, dynamics and relationship to express the original stimulus.

Abstraction in dance reduces an idea or image, say anger, to its most basic movement form. It does not copy reality but throws away some information and takes a close-up look at one small element of it which hits hard at the audience.

As you abstract and throw away material, what is left is a more focused expression of the original stimulus. Often the ideas and movements change as you work. Anna Sokolow describes how in *Rooms*

(1955) she '. . . wanted to do something about people in a big city. The theme of loneliness and non-communication evolved as I worked . . .' and in *Dreams* (1961), which was her condemnation of Nazi Germany, when she started she '. . . only had the idea of dreams, but they became nightmares and then I saw they were related to the concentration camps. Once this happened I intensified the theme by focusing on it.'[4]

Dance uses abstraction to deal with a wide range of subjects, from the fantastic images of Philippe Decouflé to the cool movement of Richard Alston. When the focus is on *pure* movement dance appears more abstract, with concern for space, time, rhythm and shape rather than plot, emotion or character.

However, dance is one of the least abstract arts because of the presence of the human figure. When watching 'pure' dance, such as in the style of Siobhan Davies or Richard Alston, audiences may feel confused because of the apparent lack of story or characters. Perhaps, instead, they can settle to enjoy seeing the dancers moving in space and time, and through various dynamics as dance for its own sake. However, the human form implies emotions, so how can viewers interpret what they see? It is interesting to consider that each viewer will make up their own individual meaning and that this is perfectly OK. Indeed often, when Davies and Alston work, they are abstracting multi-meanings from a stimulus. Watching *Wyoming* (1988) and *Soda Lake* we may see images of animal life mixed with those of landscape as well as others related to a story read aloud or the sculpture on stage. Dancer Catherine Quinn's log of rehearsals for Davies's *Wild Airs* (1999) reports making several phrases based on poetry, architecture, geometry, falling rain, slugs, bacteria and birds, as well as other phrases which just used steps in a certain rhythm with changes of direction. So when you watch such work it may well present a kaleidoscope of abstracted images all humanised, because they are human interpretations of the world around us. You can have confidence in your own abstractions as choreographer and interpretations as viewer because the interesting thing is that yours may well be different from your friends'.

As you continue to abstract and refine the phrases of your dance you will begin to choose motifs and devices to shape the overall form and structure. This *forming* process should be appropriate for the chosen

---

[4] Anna Sokolow in *The Vision of Modern Dance*, p. 110.

stimulus. The process will be a continuous reflection on, and selection of, what are the most expressive motifs in the most effective form. Remember the rule – if you don't have anything worth throwing away then you probably haven't anything worth keeping!

During the *forming* process you may begin to find an appropriate *style* for your dance. As mentioned above the '*pure*' dance style is favoured by Davies and Alston.

Task 3

➤ **Communication**

In a group view a video of Siobhan Davies's *White Man Sleeps* or an extract of a dance by Richard Alston. As you watch jot down odd words which note what *you* think about the meaning of the motifs and content of the dance.

At the end of the viewing discuss as a group the similarities and differences of opinions.

You would not confuse the music of Stravinsky with that of Debussy or Bob Marley, or the fashion designer Christian Dior with Vivienne Westwood. So it is in dance. Style is a part of everyday life: our hair, clothes, food, speech. We choose to suit our taste, but often this choice is *modified* because we do not want to appear too different from everyone else. In all arts, choice emphasises important differences, exaggerates and distorts. No two people are the same and so their styles of movement will differ. To make this clearer let us recap on dance history, which was covered in more detail in Chapter 1.

Occasionally a new style arises as a result of a strong creative individual's innovative techniques and procedures. Indeed, modern dance in the twentieth century has grown like this. As discussed previously, Nijinsky's ballets such as *L'Après Midi d'un Faune* used flat, frieze-like parallel movement inspired from Greek art and erotic gestures. Although this scandalised and shocked the ballet audiences of the time, retrospectively he is regarded as a pioneer of the modern dance genre.

Similarly the styles of Isadora Duncan, Graham and Cunningham have influenced the progress of the modern dance genre. The more you know about different styles the more your own work will be supported.

8.2 South Asian Bharatha Natyam dance

8.3 Laurie Booth and Company

8.4 Frederick Ashton as Pierrot in
CARNIVAL (1935). Notice the contrasting
looks of these different dance genres

African dance has many different styles. It travelled the world with the slave trade and developed other new styles in various countries by blending with European traditions. In this way dance genres such as tap, jazz, Latin, disco, street dance have grown. The genre of ballet has many different styles. The lyrical lines and style of English ballet, as seen in the work of Frederick Ashton, are very different to that of the harsher angles of American George Balanchine.

The post modern genre is an umbrella for a countless variety of styles. Pina Bausch and Lloyd Newson favour working with social issues, and the movement style uses physical risk and is highly emotionally charged. You can see what a contrast this is to the more lyrical, 'pure' style of Alston or Davies. Lea Anderson's style is different again as she describes here:

'If I'm trying to make a vocabulary for a dance we make strings. This is a long string of movements all in unison – a particular aesthetic. It's a language to use in that particular show. It explores a particular movement style.'

Lea Anderson[5]

Matthew Bourne and Mats Ek, in such works as their respective *Swan Lakes* (1995, 1987) use dramatic style to retell traditional stories from classical ballet, but setting them in a late twentieth century post modern society. Some of the above choreographers comment on various moral and social issues and include comic style as part of *their* styles.

Shobana Jeyasingh's style mixes genres and the dancers are accomplished in traditional Indian Bharatha Natyam, Release and Contact Improvisation. Philippe Decouflé may well require circus and acting skills from his dancers. Hans Van Manen and Jiri Kylian would require accomplishment in both classical ballet and modern dance genres for their style.

Choosing a suitable style to treat a stimulus is the key. For example if your dance was entitled *Impact and Impulse* a post modern Release improvised movement style may be suitable. Whereas if the title was *A Day in the Life of a Dolly Mixture* mixing comic and dramatic styles with a collage structure to make a dreamlike, or surreal, atmosphere would probably work best. In trying out different styles you may find

---

[5] In The Cholmondeleys Education pack.

8.5 COLD SWEAT (1990) choreography Lea Anderson for The Cholmondeleys

ones which you prefer. You could even try mixing genres which are not usually seen together, such as break dance and ballet.

Task 4

➤ **Information Technology, Problem Solving, Communication**
This task continues from Task 2.

Research your favourite choreographer and find photos, film and writings from which to identify the style. You may need to ask your teacher for help with information or visit a library. Online resources may be accessible. Now improvise in that style using appropriate music, theme, props etc. Select and shape phrases to produce a short study (max two mins).

Using the movement, photos and text that you have collected write a short talk and present it to a group.

Task 5

> ## ➤ Working With Others, Communication

By now you may have choreographed a solo. Discuss with others what makes your style special. Here is a check list of some movements which they might see:

- Travelling or staying on the spot or in a certain direction;
- Steady or impulsive;
- Gestural or whole body movement;
- Lyrical, comic, dramatic, 'pure' dance style.
- Ballet, street, jazz, African, Asian genres.

Use this discussion to learn about your strengths and weaknesses. A follow-up which you may find interesting is to compose for someone else using their own personal style.

SHAPING – REHEARSAL

The forming of the dance as a whole will continue for quite some time, especially if you are working with a group of dancers. You will reflect and refine as you rehearse, always looking to improve the expression of the stimulus which, by now, has become the content of the dance. This web of content, movement, form, structure and style will gradually melt into one, but it takes time *so* take your time. It will also need careful planning and patience with the dancers.

In order to understand the strategies needed to run rehearsals the next task may be followed.

Task 6

> ## ➤ Working With Others, Improving Your Own Learning and Performance, Communication

Collaborate, with four or five other dancers, to make a group dance for a specific type of audience eg young children or a charity. Log your *finding, choosing, shaping, rehearsing,* in a diary, keeping careful notes on dates and on the following:

- Agree on a date for the show and on a stimulus for the dance.
- Agree on a timeline with the group which works backwards from the show. Keep a copy of this.
- Delegate responsibilities for all the jobs.
- Agree on a schedule for rehearsal times and book a studio space. Keep a copy of this.
- In advance of your first rehearsal schedule make some improvisation time for yourself to prepare some movement to contribute to the group. You don't have to select accompaniment at this stage but you may prefer to do so to offer the group ideas.
- If you are planning lights, costumes, set or props ensure that the making and/or booking of them is planned into your timeline and job delegation, so that everything is ready for dress and technical rehearsals.
- Your ability to work well as a team member and be considerate of others, committed and reliable.
- Your contribution to *finding, choosing* movement or in *forming* and *shaping* the dance. Try to use dance terms to describe the movement, devices and structures that you contributed, even if they were not all used. You may use video images, photos, diagrams, text and number for these descriptions.

Working in rehearsals may involve conflicts and differences with others. It is important that when a group is choreographing collaboratively no one person dominates completely. At times you may have to be more of a dancer than a choreographer. I have *Rules Of Engagement* in my studio for these situations. One of them is that after you have put forward one idea you are not allowed to give another until everyone in the group has given one of theirs. This rule also helps those who are less extrovert to have their say. Remember, some people need support from others to encourage them to speak up.

When you are the only choreographer and your dancers look to you for movement and style the rules may differ. At first this may feel difficult because it is a big responsibility, but try to be clear about what movements and images you are using. Listen to your dancers. Do they have a problem with a certain action or a transition? Sometimes the dancers' own movements can add to your ideas so be alert to how they move. Have you considered giving structures for improvisation then choosing from what the dancers do? This could be a satisfying alternative to teaching chunks of movement. Your composition may even be based on the dancers' own special features and differences.

The quotations below reveal two choreographers' approaches to making dance and rehearsing:

'I don't prepare any movement at all until I'm in the studio. Sometimes I choreograph on my own body sometimes on theirs. It's about 50/50. I will sometimes take up a nervous mannerism of a dancer that they might do and I'll keep that and drop the steps.

After three weeks I will have got lots of strings. I start to shape them together, I might have decided on a structure.'

Lea Anderson[6]

'A lot of my work is based on improvisation. I have a specific style but I like my dancers to improvise around that as well. I like the idea of chance and the idea of experimenting [with movement].

I like learning movement but I feel more of a challenge if I have to interpret something for another person or somebody else interpret something for me.'

Helen Smith[7]

As the dance is *forming* in rehearsal everyone needs to be patient with themselves and each other. Systematic repetition of movement can be tedious and tiring, but it is the only way that dancers will build the movement memories that they need for performance, so they require sufficient time to practise. It is also the way that the choreographer can see how to refine the dance itself and how to improve the dancers' technical and expressive skills which the dance demands of them.

PERFORMANCE – DANCE APPRECIATION

In rehearsals you are engaged in a cycle of dance-making and dance appreciation. *Dance appreciation* evaluates success or failure of a dance, or a part of a dance. It is useful to evaluate your own work, or the work

---

[6] In The Cholmondeleys Education pack.
[7] www.article19.co.uk/labrats/helen.htm

of others in rehearsal or after performance. Dance critics uses this process when writing reviews. It has three stages:

1. *Describe* the movement, structure, style, accompaniment, physical setting, and dancers.
2. *Interpret* the meaning or dance content.
3. *Evaluate* the success of how 1 and 2 work together for the *context*.

In your rehearsals you will engage with all three of these stages. As you *find, choose* and *shape* movement you describe your selections and judge whether they express *(abstract/interpret)* the stimulus. Then again after the performance you may evaluate the effectiveness of your dance composition and the dancers' performance. In order to do this you should consider how suitable the dance was for the *context*. For example if your dance was designed for an audience of young children you can judge whether or not you chose stimulus, images, movement and accompaniment which kept their interest.

There are many examples of newspaper reviews which are worth researching. What do you think is the *context* of this review?

> **'Greenwich Dance Agency is not one of London's slickest theatres – its glum, local authority interior suggests that it has hosted more community socials than cutting edge shows. But Shobana Jeyasingh's new work, *[h]interland*, not only aims to re-imagine GDA's auditorium but also to transport it to an exotic cyberspace.'**
>
> *Judith Mackrell*[8]

Jeyasingh did this in a number of ways; the audience were seated on the stage using the theatre aisles, bar and balcony as stages; video footage of her dancers performing on location in London and Bangalore was projected on three large screens. She produced a performance to transform an otherwise 'unfriendly' space *(context)* for dance by imaginative placement of the audience, performers and computerised images.

Sometimes looking back in time may alter an evaluation. Much of the 1960s early post modern work in the USA was so experimental that

---

[8] *Shobana Jeyasingh* in *The Guardian* 26 October 2002

many audiences and critics hated it. Forty years later it is enjoying a successful revival. Innovation may not always lead to instant popularity in the context of its own time.

In the review below what features of the dance does the critic describe? What do you think the critic is evaluating as being successful and what as not so effective?

'These modulations from small to large, introvert to grand, breathe powerful gusts of energy through the work. But at about 75 minutes it is just too long, especially given the odd description of a textual interlude in which a story about a women in a restaurant is narrated over and over again, accumulating new information and new jokes with each version. The text was written by Caryl Churchill, and in purely formal terms it adroitly mirrors the subtle, proliferating logic of Davies's own language. The knowingness of Churchill's style, however, feels at odds with the rapt concentration of the choreography. Having broken so late into humour, *Plants and Ghosts* is left dangling in two halves.

Judith Mackrell[9]

Task 7

➤ Information Technology, Communication

This task continues from Task 6. Write a programme for your group dance performance. If you use digital video to review rehearsals you will be able to use some of the images from the film as illustrations. The programme note could include the following text:

- Title of dance.
- Short description of stimulus, content and/or themes.
- Title, performer/s and composer of accompaniment.
- Acknowledgement of other sources eg set, lighting, costume design.
- Names of choreographers and dancers.

---

[9] In *The Guardian* 23 September 2002.

Digital and computer technology can be very useful in rehearsal and performance as a means of *choosing* and *shaping* dances. Online, live video broadcast or computerised images can be used *in* performance too, as we saw with Jeyasingh's *[h]interland*. A *videodance* can even *be* the performance itself, although your examiners may not accept this just *yet*!

Since the 1970s television has taken up the idea of dance for the small screen. An early example was the 1983 *Dance on 4* series. Some of the films simply showed stage works, but others experimented with using camera and editing to adapt a stage work and make something new. The *videodance* of Richard Alston's *Plainsong* was such. Experiments included moving the cameras around in the dance. Such strategies brought the dance to life by avoiding the possible washout of the dynamic range that static cameras can produce. Perhaps you have filmed your work and noticed how it may lack the real life energy that it had in the studio. Filming and editing accommodates the viewer's eye which sees from front to back of the screen, rather than the theatre audience who view from side to side. As the technology developed *videodance* became able to create greater illusions. Sometimes allowing dancers to appear superhuman, such as the overhead shot in *Sardinas* (1990, The Cholmondeleys and The Featherstonehaughs), which transforms the white floor into a wall. The fun and illusion is that the dancers roll, slide and wriggle on a vertical surface, which of course is impossible because gravity would pull them down!

A few further examples will help you to understand some of the many possibilities. In *Boy,* there is a slow motion shot when the dancer slides down a sand dune and this really enhances the viewer's sensation of his experience. In *Downstairs,* the reckless speed which the dancers descend on pointe shoes is further heightened by blurring the film. In Decouflé's video version of *Codex,* the film is speeded up so that the running frog creatures are moving at maximum warp speed. This is not earth but some other planet far from here. Close-up is used very effectively in *Through My Eyes, A homage to Hans van Manen* (1995, Mats Ek, William Forsythe and Pina Bausch), framing isolated body parts and props so that we focus on exactly what the choreographer wishes. Superimposing images of animal limbs, computerised graphics and human form in *Deep* (1995, director Milla Moilanen) allows us to see how similar all creatures are. The choppy handheld camera in *Horseplay* (1996, Alison Murray) emphasises the everyday and playful cheek of the

8.6 FAKING IT *(1997). Motionhouse Dance Theatre, choreography Kevin Finnan, Louise Richards. Dancer Ruth Jacombes*

women. Of course a short *videodance* can also cover a wide range of locations and in this way *Cross Channel* can tell the story of one weekend break in England and France with ease. So when *videodance* is the performance we have many more choices of what to do than the usual earthbound dancing.

The advanced technologies available today are also used to create illusion in live performance too. *Faking It*, by Motionhouse Dance Company, is about power games. You can see in the photograph how a 'spin' can be put on human movement to create illusion.

Nowadays dances can be made with or for anyone across the globe. You can be an online critic of performances, or join a dance discussion group.

Task 8

➤ **Information Technology, Improving Your Own Learning and Performance, Communication**
This task continues from the log entries from Task 6.

After the performance make an evaluation of the success of your dance in discussion with your group and perhaps the audience. Log this in your working diary. Review the success of the final product and the making process. Notes may include:

- What you feel that you learnt about yourself when working in a team.
- How the movement, dance and dancers expressed the stimulus, (*describe*, *interpret*).
- How effective the dance performance was for the context, (*evaluate*).
- What would you do differently next time?

You may use text, diagrams, photographs or video images to illustrate your diary.

Being your own critic is not easy but using the process of dance appreciation in rehearsal and post performance may, over time, improve your work. It is also helpful to ask others to comment on your dances. When critiquing each others' works always have positive things to say as well as comments about things which may be improved.

The Way Ahead

In many ways each dance that you compose leaves an idea for the next one. This ongoing process always has surprises in store. One day it may even be *you* who, through study and training, discovers dance in a new way. At the least it is worth thinking about dance as being a vital part of your life – whether as dancer, choreographer, administrator or audience. Perhaps you feel that you are not destined to dance but to be a dancing engineer, flight attendant or lawyer. Whatever your occupation try to keep dance alive in your life. The world needs dancing accountants, scientists and politicians! Dance is for life – so live it!

Further Reading

Ashley, Linda *Essential Guide to Dance* (2002), Hodder & Stoughton Educational Publishers.
Ellfeldt, Lois *A Primer for Choreographers* (1974), Dance Books.
Horst, Louis and Russell, Carol (1973) Modern Dance Forms, Dance Horizons.
Morganroth, Joyce (1987) *Dance Improvisation*, University of Pittsburgh Press.
Steinman, Louise (1986) *The Knowing Body*, Shambhala.
Tufnell and Crickmay (1990) *Body, Space, Image*, Virago Press.

Video and DVD

From www.dancebooks.co.uk *A Midsummer Night's Dream*, George Balanchine. Pacific Northwest Ballet. *Black and White*, choreography by Jiri Kylian, Nederlands Dans Theatre. *Boy, Downstairs, Horseplay, Through My Eyes* and *deep*. On *The best of Springdance Cinema 96. Carmen* and *Sleeping Beauty*, Mats Ek for the Cullberg Ballet. *The Car Man*, Matthew Bourne. *L'Histoire du Soldat*, Jiri Kylian.
From www.dancing-times.co.uk *Four By Kylian. Svadebka, La Cathedrale Engloutie, Sinfonietta and Torso, Nederlands Dans Theater. Symphony in D* and *Stamping Ground*, Jiri Kylian.
From National Resource Centre for Dance: www.surrey.ac.uk/NRCD *Making of Maps* and *Romance . . . with Footsteps*, Shobana Jeyasingh.
From The Video Place; www.theplace.org.uk *Time Lapses*, Rosemary Lee peels back the layers that make a dance. On *Spring Re-Loaded 6*.

Music

Task 1 – *Electronomusic 9 Images*, John Pfeiffer, Victrola VICS 1371 RCA.

Music Useful for Improvisation

Andy Sheppard, *Introductions in the Dark*, Antilles anc. 8742.

From *Springsound; Plus Ten.*
From *New Zealand Music for Creative Dance; Worksong 3*, Don McGlashan.

Web sites

www.pina-bausch.de/
www.cullbergballet.com – Mats Ek
www.bejart.ch – Maurice Bejart, Bejart Ballet Lausanne
www.ballet.co.uk – links to dance many companies
www.cyberdance.org
www.sartorimedia.com/hands-on – interactive online dance making

GLOSSARY

Abstraction. A process of reducing something to its most basic form.

Accent. Stress on a beat or movement.

Actions. The six dance skills of travel, turn, jump, stillness, gesture and fall.

Aerobic exercise. Exercise which develops cardiovascular (of the heart) endurance and uses oxygen.

Alignment. Proper posture as near to a straight line as possible from head to toe when standing.

Asymmetry. Uneven in space, time or dynamics.

Ballet. A highly stylised technique of dance started in Europe in the 15th century.

Beat. The underlying pulse of regular movement or music.

Bounce. A small springy movement.

Canon. An overlap in the dancers' movements in time.

Centering. Bringing together the physical centre with that of the mind.

Choreography. The art of arranging movement into a meaningful whole.

Climax. The main highpoint of a dance.

Communication. The projection by the dancer to the audience of the content of the dance.

Complementary. Movements which are similar but not the same.

Contemporary dance. see Modern dance.

Content. The central idea of the dance.

Contact improvisation. Spontaneous movement to support, bounce off and onto etc a partner or group.

Contraction. Muscular shortening that changes the shape of a limb. In Graham technique contraction of the torso is a main principle.

Contrast. Movements unlike those in the main theme of a dance.

Counts. The number of beats within the measure.

Criticism. A judgement of a dance based on careful consideration of choreographic and technical principles within a specific context.

Design. Planning movement in time and space.

Development. Making complex changes to a motif so that its appearance changes noticeably.

Direction. Movement possibilities to front, back, side and the four diagonals.

Downstage. The space towards the front of the stage.

Dynamics. The variety of force, accent and quality of movement.

Effort actions. When weight, time and space are combined, eight possible ways of moving result. As identified by Rudolf Laban.

Elevation. Jumping or rising.

Enchainment. A linked series of movement.

Energy. Potential to move.

Extension. The lengthening of body parts, an important factor in a dancer's training.

Fall. A controlled movement towards the floor, either a total collapse or followed by a recovery.

Flexibility. The range of movement possible in the joints. It is important to increase this in dance training through safe stretching.

Flexion. Movement when a joint bends.

Flow. a. free or bound in movement.

b. flexible or direct through space.

c. successive or simultaneous through the body.

(As named by Rudolf Laban.)

Focus. The dancer's sight line used to increase communication with the audience.

Force. Intensity of weight, ranging from firm to light.

Form. The structure of a planned dance composition which organises the themes and motifs to produce unity.

Formation. The shape of a group of dancers eg line, circle, wedge.

Frontal plane. Gives rise to elevation.

Fugue. (in music and dance). The theme is varied and played versus itself.

Genre. An umbrella term for a type of dance. It may cover different styles of the same basic technique, eg ballet, including English and Russian styles, or African, including various styles from different parts of the continent.

Gesture. Movements which do not transfer or bear weight.

Group movement. To dance in relation to others by taking cues from each other.

Ground bass. A structure in which the basic theme is repeated in the background or other thematic movement.

Highlights. The movements of greater visual note in a dance.

Horizontal plane. Gives rise to opening and closing/turning.

Improvisation. Unplanned exploration in movement.

Isolation. Movement restricted to a single joint or muscle group, frequently used in Jazz Dance.

Jazz dance. A style of dance derived from the African slaves in the United States of America. Now often used in shows and musicals.

Jeté. A leap.

Joints. A place where two bones meet. There are four types which allow for varying amounts of movement.

Kinaesthetic. Sensing through nerves to muscles of body positions, movement and tension.

Leap. Elevation. Take off on one foot and land on the other.

Level. An aspect of space ranging from high to low through medium.

Ligament. A band of tough tissue which connects bones.

Mark. Rehearsing movement without going flat-out.

Measures. Groups of beats separated by bars into intervals.

Metre. Notes how many beats are in a measure.

Modern dance. A dance genre which emphasizes the importance of choreographers' choice of theme, intent and style.

Motif. The central movement themes of a dance which are repeated, developed and varied.

Muscle. Groups of fibres which contract and extend to produce movement.

Nervous system. The brain, spinal cord and nerves that send messages to the muscles to produce movement.

New dance. A style of dance in Britain which has evolved as a reaction against more traditional modern styles.

Opposition. A natural movement of an opposite body part to maintain balance.

Pace. The overall speed of sections of a dance.

Parallel. When standing the thighs, knees and toes facing directly forwards.

Percussive. A quality of movement which has sharp starts and stops.

Phrase. A sentence of movement of varying lengths.

Placement. Balanced alignment of level hips; legs placed in line with the hips, shoulders relaxed, spine extended, abdominal area lifted.

Plane. The result of joining two dimensions.

Plié. A bend of the knees keeping the body aligned.

Positions. The five positions of the feet in ballet, as invented in 17th century France.

Post modern dance. Started in New York in the 1960s to experiment with what dance could be.

Proscenium. The frame of the stage through which dance is seen.

Quality. This is determined by the varied use of weight and dynamics eg percussive, swings, vibrate.

Release. Letting go of tension. In Graham technique it usually follows a contraction. In new dance it is used to relax the body and mind so as to encourage ease of movement and creativity.

Relevé. Raised on half-toe.

Rhythm. A structure of movement patterns set in time.

Rotation. Movement in joints that turns around the long axis of a bone.

Sagittal. A plane which gives rise to advancing/retreating movements.

Shape. Design of body parts of one or more dancers.

Size. From small to large. An aspect of space that may be used to vary motifs.

Skeleton. The frame of bones that supports the body.

Sonata. A structure in music which uses three or four contrasting rhythms and moods that relate in tone and style.

Spotting. During turning the eyes fix on a spot and the head is quickly brought round at the last possible moment to refocus on the spot again. Avoids dizziness.

Stamina. How long the body can continue to move before exhaustion.

Stimulus. A starting point which triggers ideas for movement.

Strength. Muscle power to be increased through dance training.

Structure. An overall organised framework for a dance may be similar to those found in music, visual art or literature eg *rondo*, *collage* or *narrative*.

Style. An individual manner of choreography or performing.

Suspension. A floating, effortless light quality of movement.

Sustained. A constant, continuous smooth movement.

Swing. Pendulum-like movement with an easy natural feel.

Symmetry. Balanced or even in time, space or dynamics.

Syncopation. Stress on the beat which is not in the usual place.

Technique. Skill in dance movement.

Tempo. The speed of the movement or music.

Tendon. Tough chords which end muscles and connect them to the bones.

Transition. Links between movement themes, motifs, phrases or sections.

Travel. Moving to cover distance through the general space from point A to B.

Triplets. A three step pattern.

Turn-out. The outward rotation of the legs from the hips.

Unison. Dancers moving at the same time.

Unity. A sense of an harmonious whole in the dance form.

Upstage. The space towards the back of the stage.

Variation. A motif or theme is modified without losing its character.

Vertebrae. Single bones that make up the spine.

Vibratory. A quality of movement which is jittery-fast stops and starts.

Warm up. Muscle preparation for exercise to avoid injury.

Xylophone. A musical instrument of flat heavy wooden bars struck with a hammer.

Yoga. Hindu system of relaxation and mediation.

Zapateado. A dance with rhythmic stamping of the feet.

INDEX